HOT WHEELS PROTOTYPES

Featuring Some of the Rarest Hot Wheels in the World

Bruce Pascal

&

Michael Zarnock

A division of Lands Atlantic Publishing Co, Inc.

Lands Discovery Publishing
P.O. Box 60737
Potomac, Maryland 20854

© 2011 Bruce Pascal

All rights reserved. No part of this book may be reproduced, stored in any retrieval system, or transmitted in any form, or by any means including but not limited to electronic, mechanical, photocopy, recording, or otherwise without the written consent of the authors and publisher.

2nd Edition

ISBN 978-0-9825005-7-6

Photography: Paul M. Provencher
Editing: Kelly Lenox

Hotwheels and associated trademarks are owned by Mattel incorporated. All opinions are those of the authors and not of Mattel. The cars, documents, drawings , and artwork featured and photographed in this book are from the Bruce Pascal collection, owned by Bruce Pascal. All rights reserved.

The information in this book is true and complete to the best of our knowledge. All recommendations are made without any guarantee on the part of the author or Publisher, who disclaim any liability incurred in connection with the use of this data or specific details.

"I was not absolutely sure why Bruce wanted me to come right over to his office, but he sounded very excited and he said something about opening a large box of Hot Wheels from a former Mattel employee. As soon as I arrived Bruce started unpacking the Hot Wheels from the tissue paper. The first car was the most gorgeous orange Custom Cougar Hot Wheels we had ever seen… He continued to unpack and with each unveiling, the cars were more unique and beautiful than the next… gold OHS Custom Mustang, aqua Custom Cuda, white-interior purple Ford J-Car… All rare and in perfect condition and at that moment we knew this collection was very special…"

-Curtis Paul

Original Otto Kuhni Artwork

Harry Bradley artwork, "Hot Wheels Auto Show"

Original Hot Wheels artwork

Original Otto Kuhni artwork, Pink Beach Bomb

BRUCE PASCAL: ACKNOWLEDGMENTS

- To my wife Amy, thank you for giving me the time to pursue my passion for Hot Wheels.
- To my daughters Arielle and Carly, sorry I wouldn't let you play with my good cars.
- To my Grandfather Leo, thanks for being one of the first toy car collectors in America.
- To my parents, Brenda and Paul, thanks for showing me the joy one can get from collecting.
- To my friend Curtis Paul, thanks for reintroducing me to Hot Wheels and for your friendship.
- To my friend Sid Belzberg, thanks for making me pay more for my toys in those early eBay years.
- To Harry Bradley, your collection of drawings will be cherished always.
- To Jacobus Van Nimwegen, original owner of the Rear Load Pink Beach Bomb, thank you for your help in my early studies of the history of Hot Wheels.
- To Chris Marshall, I enjoyed learning from one of the masters.
- To Chuck Gaughan, your knowledge is immense and I am glad to call you a friend.
- To Tony Young, your name and Rear Load Beach Bombs are forever connected, thank you.
- To Sam Djujick, your name in Hot Wheels history will live on, and thanks for your friendship.
- To Dana Adams, your stories are amazing and you are an asset to the hobby.
- To the late Lawrence McCain, I will make sure the name *IDA* lives forever in Hot Wheels history.
- To my friend Derek Gable, your friendship and history lessons were invaluable.
- To Albert Baginski, I loved your history lessons.
- To Elliot Handler, thanks for creating Hot Wheels!
- To Otto Kuhni, your friendship has made my life better, and your artwork is awesome!
- To Shirley and Larry Wood, our friendship and time together provided many great memories.
- To Bob Rosas, your importance in the history of Hot Wheels is duly noted.
- To the over four hundred former Mattel employees I met and interviewed, you have enriched my life with the wonderful stories of how magical Mattel was in the early days of creating Hot Wheels.

And to Mike Zarnock, your passion for Hot Wheels is contagious; it was a pleasure working with you on this project!

MIKE ZARNOCK: ACKNOWLEDGMENTS

- As always, to my loving and dedicated wife Tina, who has so graciously put up with my obsession and the countless hours that I am away from her, including my time away from home spent on this hobby. I love you more than you will ever know and I thank you for allowing me the time to do what I do.

- To Paul Provencher, a big THANX for all these great photos!

- Bob Rosas, for his recollections of what actually happened all those years ago during the evolution of Hot Wheels, and for answering all of my endless questions.

- Derek Gable, for the great conversation we had about what went on behind the scenes at Mattel during the birth of Hot Wheels.

- And to Bruce Pascal, for asking me to be a part of this book that means so much to him. I truly appreciate the opportunity to help put this all together, not only for all of the Hot Wheels collectors current but for those to come. I learned a lot during the course of this project and I thank you from the bottom of my heart for the knowledge that I received. It's been a pleasure to work with you!

TABLE OF CONTENTS

1. INTRODUCTION
HOT WHEELS BEGINNINGS

In the collecting world, the first of anything is usually the most desirable and with Hot Wheels this rings especially true due to the toys' instant popularity. R&D cars, also called prototype or proof cars (the very first ones made) are, for many serious collectors, highly desirable and valuable. Prototypes such as the Steering Van, the Noise Making Lincoln, Over Chrome cars, and the infamous Rear Load Beach Bomb have moved from lore to legend and are some of the rarest prototypes known.

Walt Boriak, who was a retail wholesaler from 1967-1994 and supplied many of the 25,000-plus toy dealers across the country with Hot Wheels, stated, "The product [Hot Wheels] sold so fast they [Mattel] knew they had a winner on their hands. Most all the inventory was sold even before it left the back store room!"

But the prototype story doesn't actually start here. It starts back in the late 1960s at the Mattel studio with Elliot Handler, co-owner of Mattel, and his engineering team. Handler wanted to get into the hot die-cast toy market. The task seemed daunting because Matchbox by Lesney, Corgi, Dinky, Husky, and even Tootsietoys were already making toy cars. His advisers indicated that he was crazy to even try to compete in the flooded market. But he was determined to introduce a new boy's toy that would rival his wife Ruth's toy creation eight years earlier, the Barbie doll.

Sticking to his guns, Elliot knew that if he made a toy car that had better "play value" than the competition, Mattel would be successful. Play value is something that keeps a child interested enough to continually play with a toy. He knew that children would rather play with fast rolling cars than slow rolling, thick-axled ones that have to be continually pushed. That, combined with California styling, would be the key to beating the competition.

American automobiles with bigger, wider tires and radical paint jobs were all the rage. Leading the pack were Mustangs, Camaros, Firebirds, and Corvettes, which gained muscle and speed during this time period. Car enthusiasts were also modifying stock cars to look cool and stand out on the street. Mattel wanted to use the same concepts when it came to designing their new die-cast toy cars.

One morning, late in 1966, in a Research & Development meeting, Elliot Handler held up a Matchbox car and announced, "We should make these cars… but better!" In attendance were Bernie Loomis, marketing VP and head of Mattel's Boys' Toys department; Jack Ryan, head of the Preliminary Design group; and project engineer Jack Malek. After about an hour of heated discussion with all the naysayers, Elliot walked to the door of the meeting room and said, "Why not we try?"

Jack Ryan, whose previous job was with Raytheon as an electrical engineer, told his engineering team to go make a fast-rolling toy car and not to come back until they had something good. Using existing toy cars from local toy stores and parts from the Mattel shop, his team got right to work. They found ten thousand feet of unused mandolin wire from another toy project and used about two inches of it for the prototype wheel axles. Jack thought that if the axles were thinner than those of existing die-cast cars, the decreased friction would allow the wheels to spin much faster. Later on in the design process, head engineer Howard Newman took the idea and developed the axle into a fully independent torsion bar suspension, whereby each wheel could move up and down independently just like real cars. He also added the use of Delrin™, a very hard plastic material, for the inner wheel cylinders, making a low-resistance bearing that would fit snugly into the wheel housing.

Believe it or not, several hours later the preliminary design group called Elliot just as he was leaving for the day. Back in Elliot's office Loomis placed a toy car on the desk in front of Handler. Jack Malek lightly flicked the car with his finger and the prototype rolled across Elliot's rather large desk, off the edge, and onto the floor. Legend has it that at this point Elliot looked up to Jack and said, "That is some hot wheels!" The design team did not realize it then, but this early prototype model was the beginning of one of the most prolific toys to come along in decades; soon it would become the best selling toy car on the market.

Earliest known sketch of Hot Wheels prototype Custom Fleetside (1967)

Custom Camaro sketch (1967); note the exaggerated rake of the car

Custom Cougar sketch (1967)

The following photos show preliminary test cars that were constructed from an array of parts lying around the factory or from other manufacturers. These cars are truly one-of-a-kind.

The earliest known examples of Hot Wheels prototypes are a red Matchbox Mustang and green Matchbox Indy Car (1967). The Mustang is a modified Matchbox car with smoothed surfaces, painted body, and bumpers.

The hand-tooled base of the Custom Mustang (1967)

Both cars were made from modified Matchbox cars, with a hand-tooled "blank" base and 5-spoke Cragar-type wheels, and painted; note the hardware store screws on the base of the Brabham-Repco F1

2. THE WHO, WHAT, WHERE, AND WHY

THE PROTOTYPE R & D CARS

Getting the green light to move forward on the new Hot Wheels project, Mattel hired real car engineers and former Ford and Chevy car designers to design and develop a toy car that would retail for fifty-six cents.

Two key additions to the Mattel group were Paul Peterson and Harry Bentley Bradley. Paul started with Mattel in late 1965 as an apprentice model maker. As the low man on the totem pole, he was instructed to hand-make many of the first Hot Wheels prototypes. Harry, a designer from General Motors hired by Mattel in 1966, would go on to design the first collection of sixteen cars, and may also have inspired Elliot Handler's idea to make "hot" cars. Harry had a customized 1964 El Camino built by Detroit's Alexander Brothers with hotrod redline tires, five-spoke mag wheels, shiny gold candy-colored paint, side pipes, and a black tonneau cover on the rear bay. Harry regularly parked his pride and joy right outside the main door to the Mattel offices. It was the epitome of the California look for cars in the day.

MY CUSTOMIZED 64 EL CAMINO IN HERMOSA BEACH, 1966. I TURNED THIS INTO THE CUSTOM FLEETSIDE, ONE OF THE ORIGINAL 16 HOT WHEELS THAT I DESIGNED IN THE WINTER OF 66-67. THE EL CAMINO INSPIRED THE HOT WHEELS "LOOK": 5-SPOKE MAG WHEELS, RED STRIPE WIDE OVAL TIRES, A STYLIZED POWER DOME ON THE HOOD, BRIGHT CANDY COLORS AND A STRONG CALIFORNIA CUSTOM CAR IMAGE. THIS FORMAT LED TO THE EVENTUAL INCLUSION OF RADICAL REAL-LIFE CUSTOM SHOW CARS.

Harry Bentley Bradley ©11-21-01

The unique process of designing fast-moving toy cars was actually an art form and required a lot of talented personnel. The design team quickly began producing prototypes and test models to refine the movement of the toy cars and designing the car bodies, undercarriage (base), and wheels.

In the case of Hot Wheels cars, there were actually two preliminary design groups: a department of Mattel employees and a department of specialty sub-contractors. Both were located in the Mattel building, but they worked separately. This format created great competition between the two departments, keeping everyone on their toes and the ideas flowing. Having these two think tanks in one building was kind of like having the C.I.A. and the F.B.I. under the same roof. They were very competitive and tried to keep their development secrets from each other until it was time to unveil them.

Model maker Lester Stormon's Mattel employee lab badges

To quote Derek Gable, who ran a large part of the department from 1968 to 1984, "The purpose of Preliminary Design was to provide the company with hundreds of new concepts whereby only a few were taken to market each year. New ideas were developed to a point where they could be presented to management on a bi-weekly basis. The presentations consisted of Prototypes that demonstrated the function of the idea, renderings that demonstrated the visuals, cost estimates and marketing concepts." Derek Gable is credited with many popular and collectible Hot Wheels accessory designs. Among the more notable are the Sky Show Set, Speedometer, and the Hot Shots.

The original cost of making a single Hot Wheels car was forty-eight cents; it retailed for a mere fifty-six cents with an average manufacturing scrap loss rate of thirty percent. Any imperfection in the die cast affected paint quality. Bad wheels due to cracking were also problematic and many had to be replaced before leaving the factory floor. During the first six-month period of making Hot Wheels, production increased tenfold, reaching over one million cars per week at each manufacturing plant. Seymour Adler, Vice President of Operations, was credited with reducing the scrap loss rate to five percent, improving the wheel molds, implementing inventory control, and introducing manufacturing night shifts, all of which would ultimately bring down the cost of a car to twenty-seven cents for the time period.

The "prelim design" is also where many play value ideas came together. Again, play value was a very important concept to Elliot Handler along with, of course, the toys' aesthetics and practicality. Track and play sets came into the picture at this time, dramatically increasing the play value of the Hot Wheels toy. The people in the prelim design departments were basically the inventors of many Hot Wheels accessories. These designers would come up with ideas and then seek to build their ideas with miscellaneous parts.

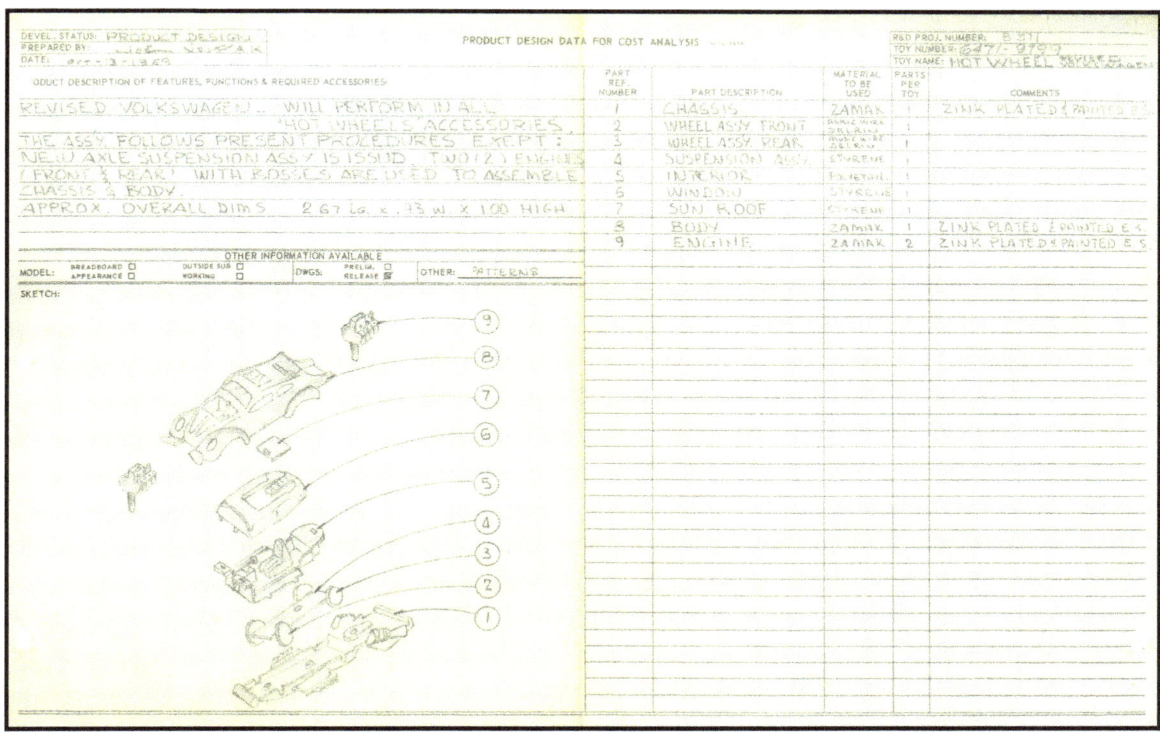

PRODUCT DESIGN DATA FOR COST ANALYSIS

DEVEL. STATUS: PRODUCT DESIGN
PREPARED BY:
DATE:

R&D PROJ. NUMBER: 5311
TOY NUMBER: 6471-9799
TOY NAME: HOT WHEEL

ODUCT DESCRIPTION OF FEATURES, FUNCTIONS & REQUIRED ACCESSORIES:

REVISED VOLKSWAGEN.. WILL PERFORM IN ALL 'HOT WHEELS' ACCESSORIES. THE ASSY FOLLOWS PRESENT PROCEDURES EXEPT: NEW AXLE SUSPENSION ASSY IS ISSUD. TWO (2) ENGINES (FRONT & REAR) WITH BOSSES ARE USED TO ASSEMBLE CHASSIS & BODY.
APPROX. OVERALL DIMS 2.67 LG. x .93 W. x 1.00 HIGH

PART REF. NUMBER	PART DESCRIPTION	MATERIAL TO BE USED	PARTS PER TOY	COMMENTS
1	CHASSIS	ZAMAK	1	ZINK PLATED & PAINTED E.S.
2	WHEEL ASSY FRONT	[illegible]	1	
3	WHEEL ASSY REAR	[illegible]	1	
4	SUSPENSION ASSY	STYRENE	1	
5	INTERIOR	[illegible]	1	
6	WINDOW	STYRENE	1	
7	SUN ROOF	STYRENE	1	
8	BODY	ZAMAK	1	ZINK PLATED & PAINTED E.S.
9	ENGINE	ZAMAK	2	ZINK PLATED & PAINTED E.S.

OTHER INFORMATION AVAILABLE
MODEL: BREADBOARD ☐ APPEARANCE ☐ OUTSIDE SUB ☐ WORKING ☐
DWGS: PRELIM. ☐ RELEASE ☒
OTHER: PATTERNS

SKETCH:

Very early product cost analysis for Evil Weevil (1970)

Fred Adickes, Mattel's Chief of Industrial Design, who previously designed cars for Chrysler, went home one night soon after the R&D team started working on the new Hot Wheels, thinking about the ability of his son's Pinewood Derby to roll quickly down a track.

Following this same concept, he gathered up 15 feet of unused flexible plastic garage weather stripping and brought it in to work the next day. Adickes C-clamped the end of the weather stripping to his desk and first sent down a regular Matchbox, which just happened to fit inside the edges of the weather strip, and as expected, it rolled to the end of the track. Then, he took the new prototype Hot Wheels car and sent it down the prototype track. It raced down and kept on going, across the office floor, all the way down the hallway, finally hitting the wall where it stopped. This early prototype strip seemed innocent enough, but this simple track was the beginning of Hot Wheels accessories.

Shell gas station attendant button (1973)

In many cases these early accessories and prototype cars would make even Frankenstein look attractive, with their mismatched colors and crudely handmade parts. Perhaps these inventors and designers felt a little like Dr. Frankenstein when their creations came to life!

There was even a time in 1971 when both design groups simultaneously came up with two very similar ideas about how a toy car could be propelled. The two concepts were very good individually, similar in design, but slightly different in functionality. The problem was that only one could be used. A race was planned to determine which of the two prototypes was faster; the winner would have their concept used in the final design. Everyone got together to watch the race between the two different departments, including Elliot Handler, who would witness the winner.

This race was for the new Hot Shots Hot Wheels. The pull-string motor (Derek's and Jack's group) won, over a gyro rotation-type application. The pull string's momentum lasted longer and was more constant in speed than the gyro, which had a quicker start but lost momentum as the race went on. This type of event fostered an enjoyable and creative work environment between the creative groups and filtered out to all the other Mattel employees. Mr. Handler would often drop by one of the employee's offices, peek in, and ask, "What are you working on?" The engineer would pull out a concept piece and he and Mr. Handler would get down on their hands and knees and play on the floor.

Mattel employees (mid-1970s)

Employee working on the early blister pack packaging designed by Rick Irons

A lot of ideas flowed through the preliminary design departments, some good, some not so good. But all had to go through the important review process to meet both the price point and play value guidelines. One of the more interesting attempts at new product ideas included toy cars with little working steering wheels that could potentially make the car turn. The steering cars were a great concept, but did not pass the review process.

Hot Wheels were designed to race down long tracks that might have turns attached to them. This and the fact that the working steering wheels were not cost effective sealed the fate of the steering cars and vans. For this reason, only a few of these prototypes are known to exist.

Steerable Continental Mark III with tool shop-made base

Steerable Continental Mark III prototype (*above* and *below*)

Prototype steerable Hot Wheels Super Van (*above* and *below*), designed and hand built by Derek Gable; note the small plastic figure driving the van

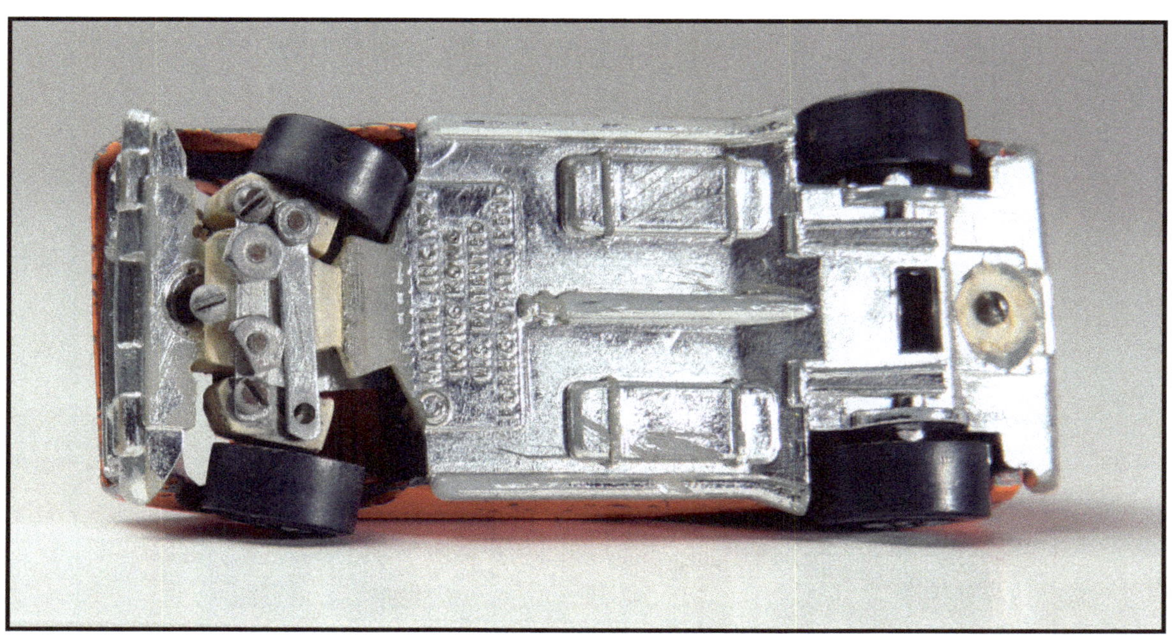

The R&D think tank also engineered some prototype cars that made noises, such as engine sounds, sirens, or squealing tires. To achieve these sounds a loop of tape with a phonograph needle similar to an early gramophone was engineered. As the car wheels moved along the floor, the back axle would roll the tape and the needle would ride the printed sound track, producing the sound.

Noise-making Continental Mark III base (*above* and *below*) with red tape that would make sounds as the car rolled

It is noteworthy that many of the noise-maker prototypes were made using the larger car body castings such as Lincoln Continentals or vans. This made it possible for the extra components to fit inside. However, these models, along with the steering cars, could not be sold at the retail level for less than one dollar each, so they never made it to production.

Noise-making Continental Mark III (*above* and *below*)

Early prototype of a Flip Out car — it could roll and then "flip out. " This concept was put into production about ten years after this prototype.

Unusual colors were sometimes used for these prototype pieces that were not used in any of the actual production pieces. Some think that these colors were used to bring attention to the unique prototype piece; others speculate that it was just the color of paint that had been loaded in the paint machine at the time.

Early prototype of a Flip Out car in action

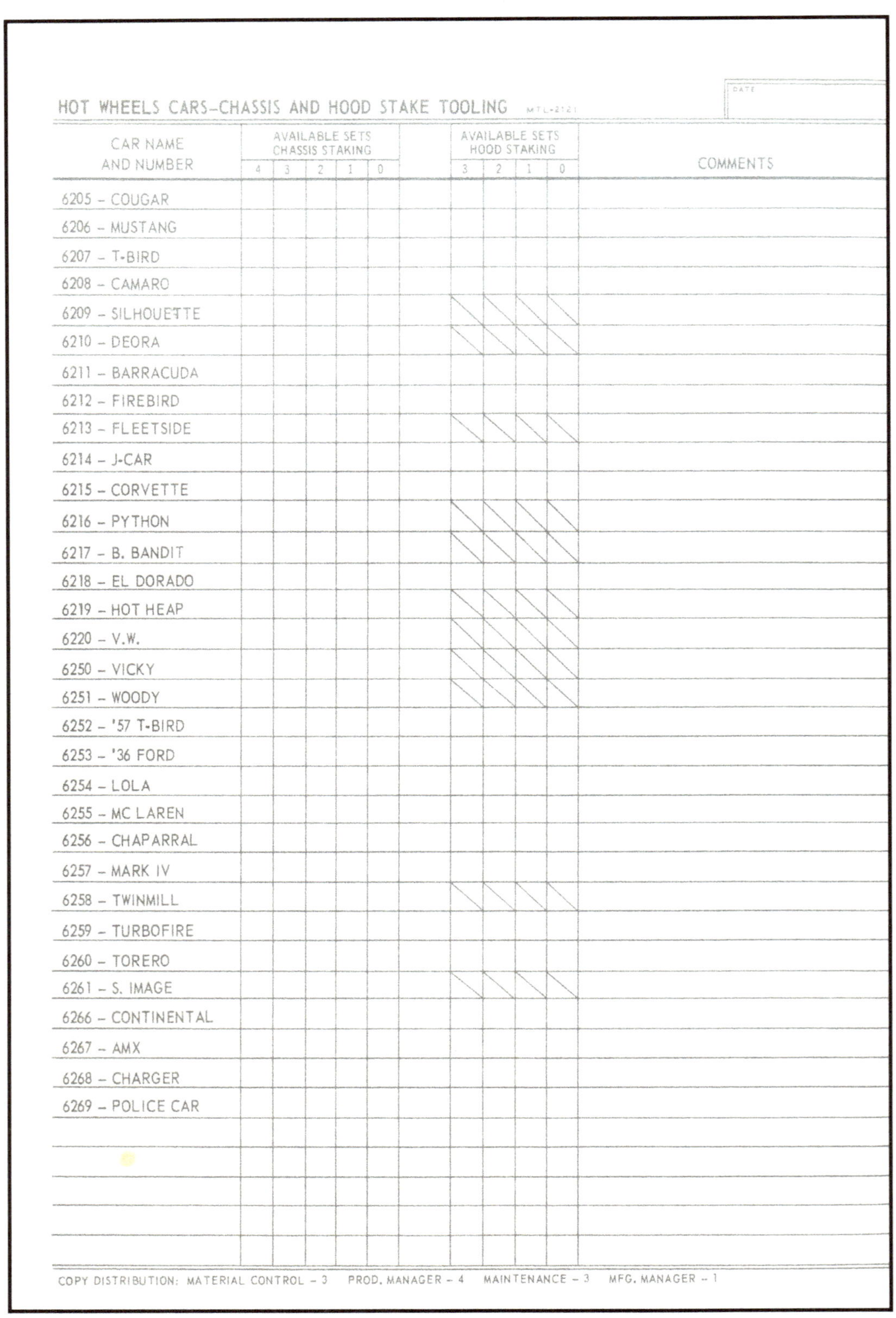

HOT WHEELS CARS–CHASSIS AND HOOD STAKE TOOLING MTL-2121

DATE

CAR NAME AND NUMBER	AVAILABLE SETS CHASSIS STAKING						AVAILABLE SETS HOOD STAKING				COMMENTS
	4	3	2	1	0		3	2	1	0	
6205 – COUGAR											
6206 – MUSTANG											
6207 – T-BIRD											
6208 – CAMARO											
6209 – SILHOUETTE							\	\	\	\	
6210 – DEORA							\	\	\	\	
6211 – BARRACUDA											
6212 – FIREBIRD											
6213 – FLEETSIDE							\	\	\	\	
6214 – J-CAR											
6215 – CORVETTE											
6216 – PYTHON							\	\	\	\	
6217 – B. BANDIT							\	\	\	\	
6218 – EL DORADO											
6219 – HOT HEAP							\	\	\	\	
6220 – V.W.							\	\	\	\	
6250 – VICKY							\	\	\	\	
6251 – WOODY							\	\	\	\	
6252 – '57 T-BIRD											
6253 – '36 FORD											
6254 – LOLA											
6255 – MC LAREN											
6256 – CHAPARRAL											
6257 – MARK IV											
6258 – TWINMILL							\	\	\	\	
6259 – TURBOFIRE											
6260 – TORERO											
6261 – S. IMAGE							\	\	\	\	
6266 – CONTINENTAL											
6267 – AMX											
6268 – CHARGER											
6269 – POLICE CAR											

COPY DISTRIBUTION: MATERIAL CONTROL – 3 PROD. MANAGER – 4 MAINTENANCE – 3 MFG. MANAGER – 1

Hot Wheels cars chassis and hood stake tooling chart

Interestingly, Sam Djujick, who was in charge of production testing and had an industrial engineering degree, figured out that black-painted cars showed faults better than other colors, therefore many early test cars were painted black. After these prototypes completed all the stages in R&D, they went to "the morgue." Sadly, many of these pieces of Hot Wheels history were taken apart, possibly to make other toy car prototypes, or to be thrown away.

Prototype Mercedes-Benz C111 painted black; notice that the steering wheel mechanism in the windshield is actually a redline hot wheel (*next page*)

Early run Indy Eagle test cars

3. MOCK-UP MODEL
PLASTIC AND WOOD PROTOTYPES

Hong Kong model shop (1967)

It was June 1967 and the first sixteen Hot Wheels designs had been chosen, but the cars still needed to be manufactured. Because it was difficult for the model maker to carve the molds in the 1/64 scale and retain sharp details, larger industry-standard 4X models were made first and then scaled down to preserve the detail. In the hands of a carver, just one 4X scale wood model could take as much as 400 hours to make.

With fast-approaching deadlines, Mattel needed to make the models as quickly as possible. A solution was found at Ruby's Toyland, 951 South La Brea Avenue in Inglewood, California. Harry Bradley went to Ruby's and bought several model kits, including AMT's The Silhouette, Chevy Fleetside, Chevy Truck, Ford J Car, Firebird, and others, and had the cars assembled by the skilled Mattel model makers. Now Mattel had the cars, but in 1/25 scale. To make the Chevy Fleetside, Harry's model maker used two car kits, one from a Chevy Truck and one from a Chevy car. This one-of-a-kind aqua model is the earliest known Hot Wheels scale model.

Prototype Chevy Fleetside plastic model sitting on body detail plans (1967)

The first ever model of the Hot Wheels Concept Custom Fleetside made from several 1/25 AMT plastic model kits purchased at Ruby's Toy Store in 1967

Production speed was further improved with the use of a pantograph machine, which could take a larger model and then recreate it identically in a different scale, such as the 1/64 scale used for Hot Wheels.

The pantograph machine was used to trace and then scale down (using a special mechanical linkage based on parallelograms) either a wood or epoxy model that was, on average, four times the size of a normal Hot Wheels car.

Jack Hargraves works with the panagraph to reduce a large wooden model of a car to a smaller plastic prototype.

Jack Hargraves working on the pantograph machine from

***The Model Shop – Toymaker's Laboratory* (1971)**

Courtesy of Machine Tool Traders

The pantograph machine (pictured above) was like a modern CNC milling machine, but with a whole lot more set-up and teardown time involved. Instead of using a computer program to cut the image, the wooden or epoxy pattern was placed on one side and a block of brass on the other. The technician would start by setting a stylus on the model and a cutter blade on the other end. As the stylus went along the body of the model on one side, it would cut the shape from the solid block of brass on the other. This process would usually start at the top. Once the top was cut, they would have to break down the set up and start over with the pattern and the brass block laid on one side and then cut the top surface. This process would have to be done for both sides, the top and bottom, and the front and rear. The body would then be hollowed out with a scraping tool. After the cutting, the parts would be polished and detailed.

Quarles 1st to Complete Model Maker Program

Model maker Johnson Quarles checks the final configuration of a model he has made for a new Mattel toy — a model used in designing the tools to make production toys of the model's precise shape. Quarles is the first to complete Mattel's apprenticeship program in model making under the Division of Apprenticeship Standards, State of California.

©1969 Mattel, Inc./Hawthorne, Calif. 90250/Printed in U.S.A.

Making models as a hobby led to making models as a career for Johnson Quarles in R&D. The thing that confuses some people is that they're altogether different kinds of models.

Johnny, as his colleagues call him, is a builder of radio-controlled model aircraft of considerable repute. He has developed techniques for making airplanes which are flown by radio that have got him on the cover of a national magazine and are considered years ahead of their time.

But that isn't what makes him special around Mattel. His repute on the job lies in the fact that he is the first graduate of Mattel's apprenticeship program for model makers.

The program, established under the Division of Apprenticeship Standards of the State of California in 1968, involves four years of apprenticeship. When he got in, Johnny Quarles was given 36 months credit on the four years because of prior work he had done in the field.

Johnny's first efforts in this area were made when he was 10, making model cars and airplanes. His talent soon led him into more sophisticated territory, and he began making radio-controlled aircraft as a hobby and later professionally.

But skilled as he was, he still felt the need for formal training in order to broaden his capabilities. A graduate of Los Angeles High School, he studied at the Art Center College of Design, and later came to Mattel where he went through the apprenticeship program.

Right now he has two jobs — making models for future Mattel toys and working with engineers in designing tools with which to make those toys of the future.

He's married; he and his wife, June, have a 6-year-old son whom Johnny describes as a red-hot Hot Wheels fan. Despite his skill at making toys, Johnny doesn't make any for the youngster.

"At his age," he says, "they'd last five minutes. It's better to let him play with production toys. They last."

EXTRA! EXTRA!

In the last issue of Toymakers Topics, you learned about Mattel's biggest-ever Christmas promotion "Extra Special Life". Enclosed with this issue is the "Extra" of the promotion, the Toy Book!

16 Pages in full color, the Book is the most powerful single piece of toy advertising ever done anywhere, by anyone. The Toy Book will be delivered with the Sunday paper on Nov. 16 to 28,500,000 homes all across the country (Delivered in New York and Pittsburgh on Nov. 9). Planned just in time for Christmas shopping, the Toy Book will presell the complete Mattel and Monogram lines to 85,500,000 kids and adults. Your advance copy of the Toy Book will give you a preview of the Christmas shopping yet to come for us adults and provide many hours of delightful reading for our children!

Johnson Quarles master wood carver article (1969)

The model shop at Mattel had about sixty-five employees in 1968, but only a few were master carvers. Jack Hargraves, known for being a fast carver, worked on many new models, using maple wood, along with Johnson Quarles, the carver for both the Maserati Mistral and the original Rear Loader Beach Bomb. Quarles, who was part of a special minority training program at Mattel, is now an airline pilot in Alaska, but still remembers the tremendous hours and effort necessary to carve just those two models.

What-4 prototype, 4X carved wood model, and original plans

Because of the numerous models being designed at Mattel and the limited number of carvers, Mattel went outside of its own shop and hired a firm called International Design Affiliates (IDA) to help create the wooden models. It was not uncommon for employees of Mattel to leave Mattel and then work for IDA and vice-versa. Most of the Sizzler Cars™ and Chopcycles™ were prototyped at IDA, as were numerous cars after 1969, starting with the Mad Maverick (soon called the Mighty Maverick). Many ex-employees tell tales of how the wood carvings were eventually lost or even used as firewood; the remaining few are rare pieces of Mattel Hot Wheels history.

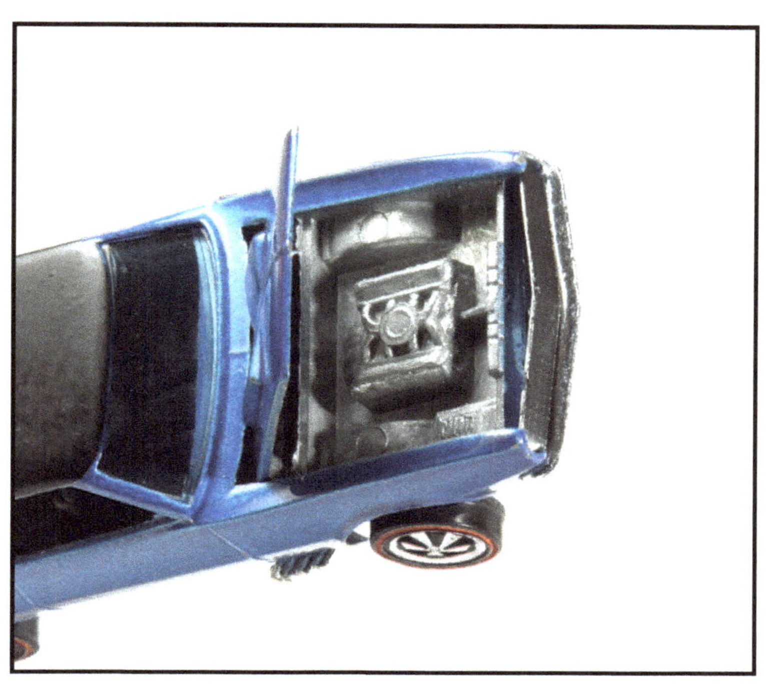

One of the first prototype Custom Camaros with early engine design

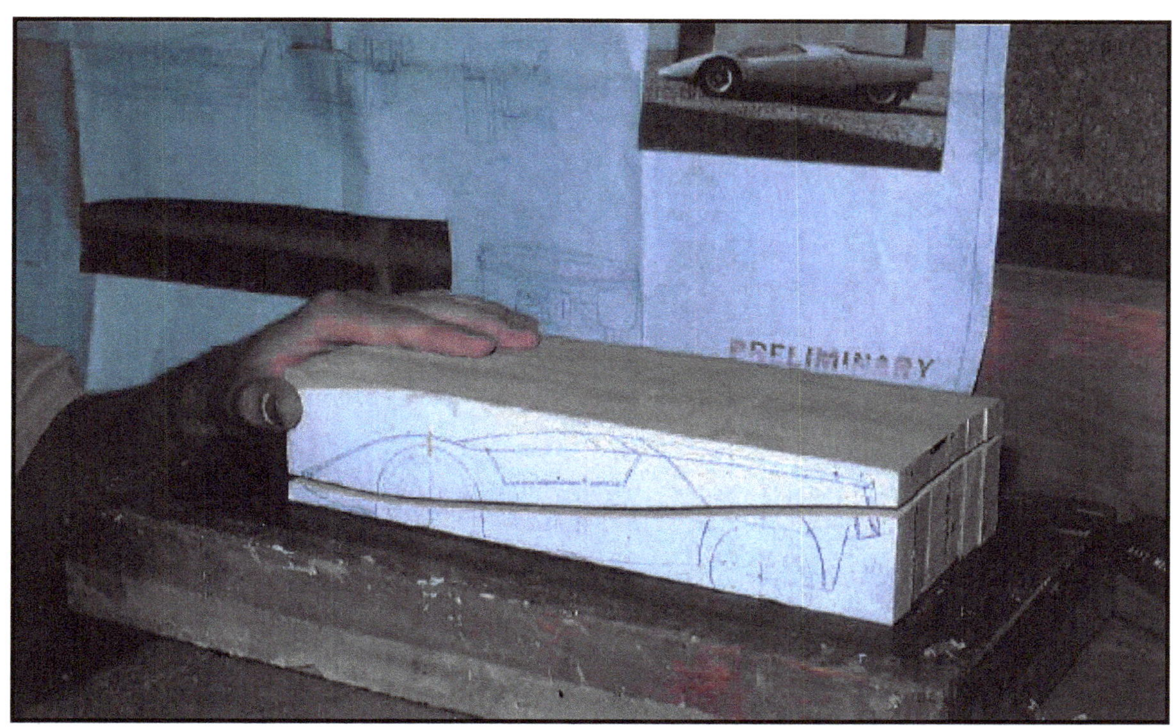

Wood block pre-carving for Ferrari 512S

The seven-piece wood model for S'Cool Bus

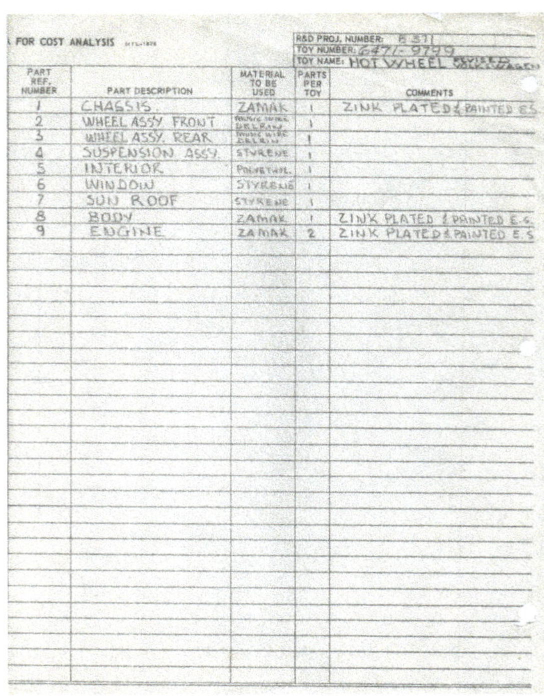

FOR COST ANALYSIS

R&D PROJ. NUMBER: B 371
TOY NUMBER: 6471-9799
TOY NAME: HOT WHEEL REVISED VOLKSWAGEN

PART REF. NUMBER	PART DESCRIPTION	MATERIAL TO BE USED	PARTS PER TOY	COMMENTS
1	CHASSIS.	ZAMAK	1	ZINK PLATED & PAINTED E.S.
2	WHEEL ASSY FRONT	MUSIC WIRE DELRIN	1	
3	WHEEL ASSY. REAR	MUSIC WIRE DELRIN	1	
4	SUSPENSION ASSY.	STYRENE	1	
5	INTERIOR	POLYETHYL.	1	
6	WINDOW	STYRENE	1	
7	SUN ROOF	STYRENE	1	
8	BODY	ZAMAK	1	ZINK PLATED & PAINTED E.S.
9	ENGINE	ZAMAK	2	ZINK PLATED & PAINTED E.S

General Hot Wheels cost analysis spreadsheet

Hong Kong model shop (1967); notice the plastic shavings on the floor and the 1967 model box kit on the workbench shelf

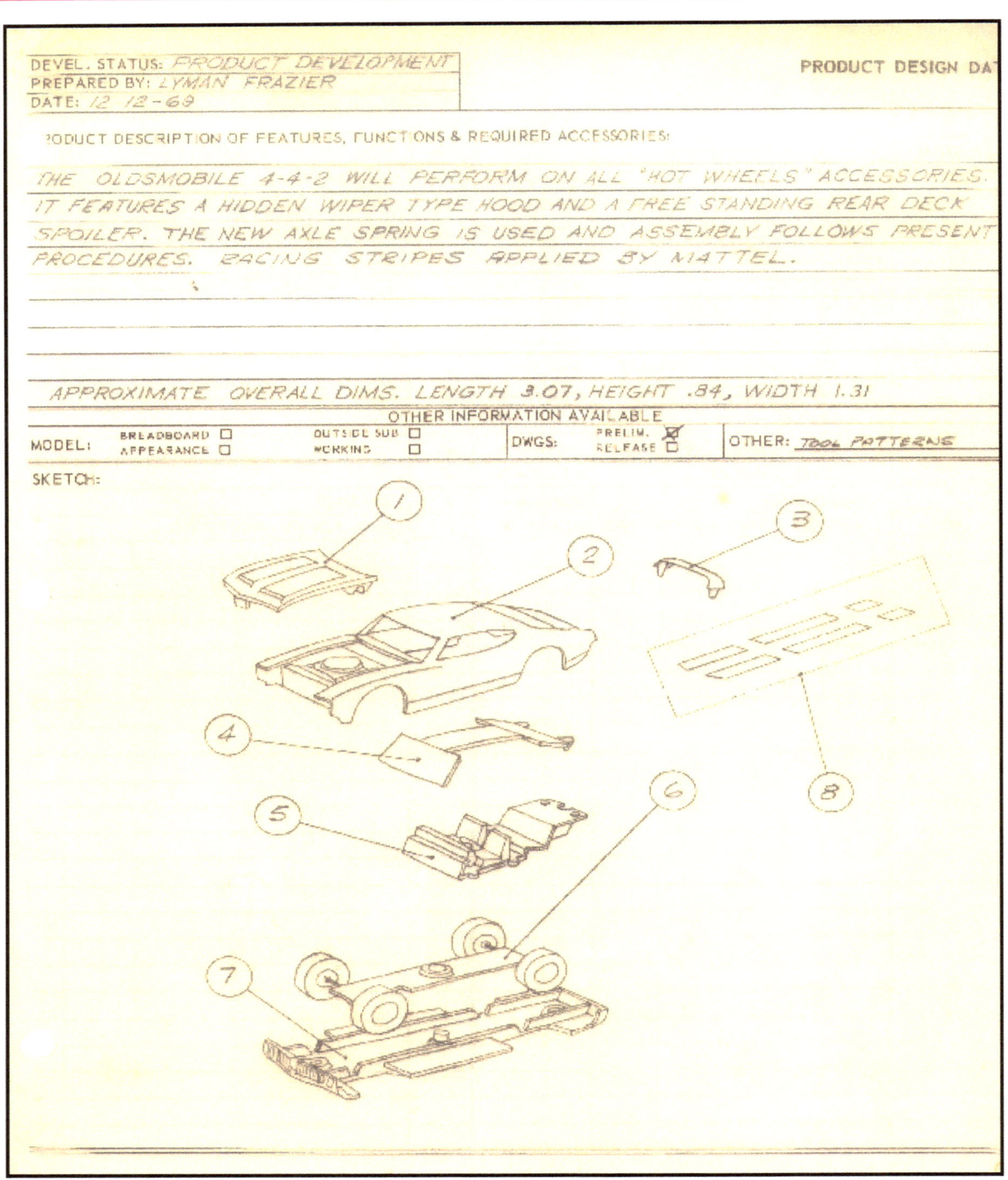

DEVEL. STATUS: PRODUCT DEVELOPMENT
PREPARED BY: LYMAN FRAZIER
DATE: 12 12-69

PRODUCT DESIGN DA

?ODUCT DESCRIPTION OF FEATURES, FUNCTIONS & REQUIRED ACCESSORIES:

THE OLDSMOBILE 4-4-2 WILL PERFORM ON ALL "HOT WHEELS" ACCESSORIES. IT FEATURES A HIDDEN WIPER TYPE HOOD AND A FREE STANDING REAR DECK SPOILER. THE NEW AXLE SPRING IS USED AND ASSEMBLY FOLLOWS PRESENT PROCEDURES. RACING STRIPES APPLIED BY MATTEL.

APPROXIMATE OVERALL DIMS. LENGTH 3.07, HEIGHT .84, WIDTH 1.31

OTHER INFORMATION AVAILABLE

MODEL: BREADBOARD ☐ APPEARANCE ☐ OUTSIDE SUB ☐ WORKING ☐ | DWGS: PRELIM. ☒ RELEASE ☐ | OTHER: TOOL PATTERNS

SKETCH:

Product development analysis for the Olds 442 (1969)

Mock-up drawing of the Allison Gremlin (Open Fire)

Mock-up drawing of the Cyclone (never made)

Painted wood model of the Ferrari 512S

Color hand drawing of the Side Kick: notice the I.D.A stamp on the right

Resin casting boat and Seasider; the engine is not the production version

Prototype Seasider with clear plastic interior and production engine

Porsche 917 with early plaster of Paris mold

Hard resin model with Mercedes-Benz 280SL Hot Wheels

Sculpted wood model with What-4 Hot Wheels

Brabham-Repco F1 early prototype with sculpted model

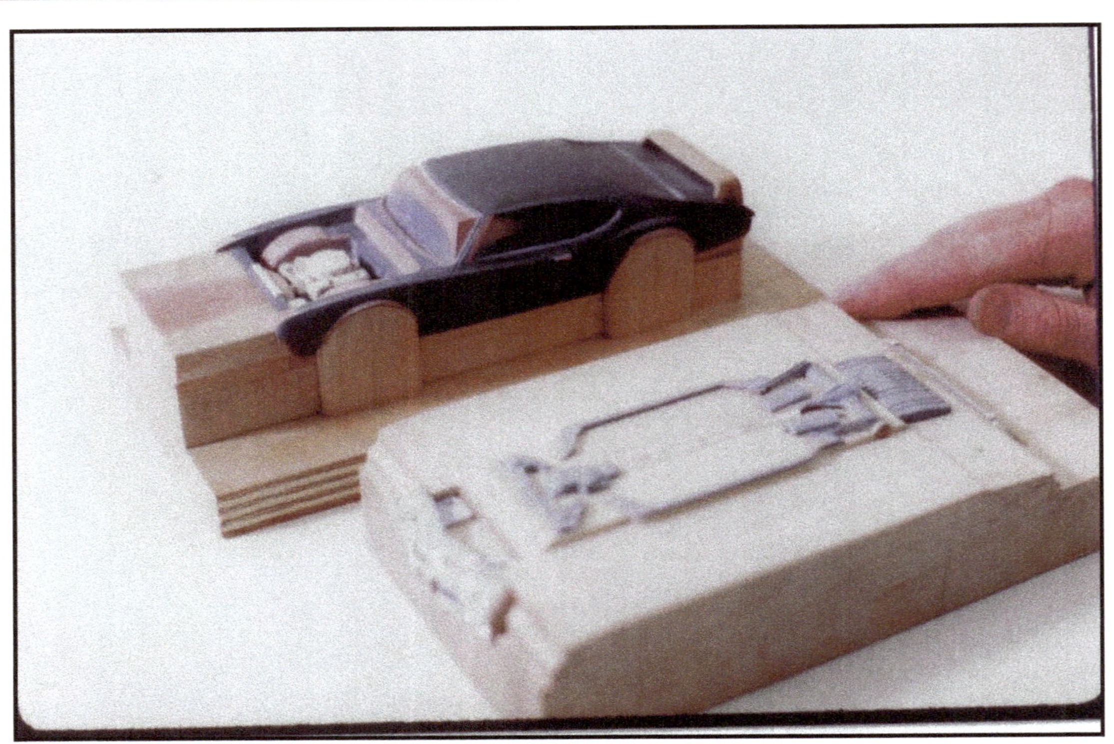

Sculpted wood model plate for Olds 442

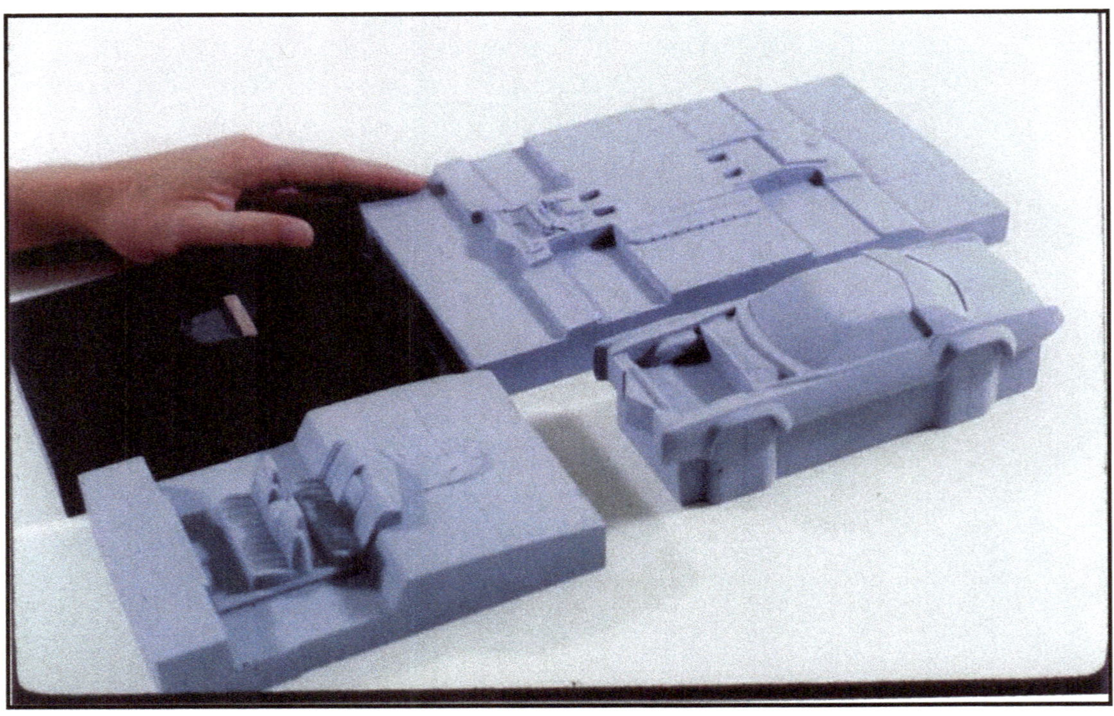

Sculpted hard resin model for Sugar Caddy, with interior and base

FOR COST ANALYSIS MTL-1876

R&D PROJ. NUMBER: 8522
TOY NUMBER: 6467
TOY NAME: OLDSMOBILE 4-4-2

PART REF. NUMBER	PART DESCRIPTION	MATERIAL TO BE USED	PARTS PER TOY	COMMENTS
1	HOOD	ZAMAK	1	PLATED-STAKED TO BODY-PAINT WITH BODY
2	BODY	ZAMAK	1	PLATED-ELECTRO-STATIC PAINTED
3	SPOILER	STYRENE	1	PRESS FIT WITH BODY
4	WINDOW	G.P. STYRENE	1	
5	INTERIOR	POLYETHYLENE	1	FOLD-UP DASH & STEERING WHEEL
6	SUSPENSION ASSEMBLY	HI-IMPACT STYRENE	1	
	AXLE-LONG } FRONT	MUSIC WIRE	1	
	RIM-MED. } FRONT	DELRIN	2	
	HUB-MED. } FRONT	STYRENE	2	
	AXLE-LONG } REAR	MUSIC WIRE	1	
	RIM-LARGE } REAR	DELRIN	2	
	HUB-LARGE } REAR	STYRENE	2	
7	CHASSIS	ZAMAK	1	PLATED
8	LABEL - RACING STRIPES	ACETATE	1	APPLIED BY MATTEL

Cost analysis for Olds 442 (*above*) and sculpted wood model (*below*)

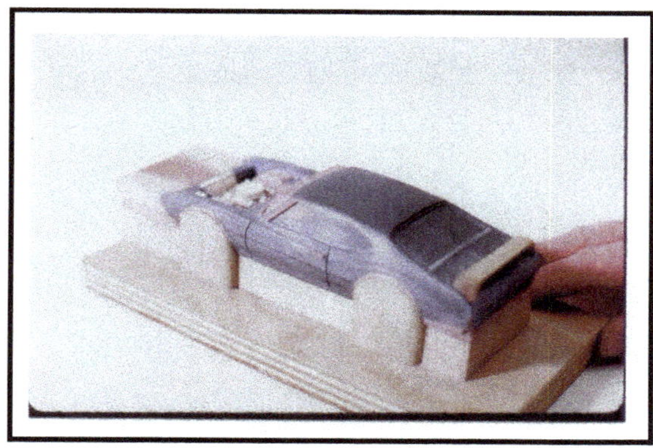

4. ALTERNATIVE METALLURGY
THE BRASS CARS

Brass cars truly define the prototype Hot Wheels. These cars were painstakingly carved from a block of solid brass directly from the model maker's patterns. Again, the pantograph machine was used to trace then scale down the larger pattern to the 1/64 scale* toy car. Because brass prototypes required over 200 hours of fabrication, usually only one replica was made for each model car.

Brass Olds 442, also used for the catalog photo

* It's interesting to note that the brass prototype was 1/65 scale rather than the 1/64 scale used as the actual production scale of the Hot Wheels toy car.

These prototypes were extremely close in size and weight to the final manufactured ZAMAC* zinc alloy car, so they were also ideal for track and Super Charger testing. They rolled and move in similar fashion to the ZAMAC cars, so if the brass car didn't work properly on a Hot Wheels track set, it gave Mattel a chance to rectify the problem before the ZAMAC car went into production. The brass differed from the ZAMAC in that tooling modifications could be made to the brass car whereas the ZAMAC was poured into molds and could crumble easily upon tooling modification. If a car needed modifications after testing, it was far less work and money to modify the existing brass car than to make an entirely new ZAMAC piece mold.

Prototype brass Mighty Maverick on IDA product definition plans (1969)

*The bodies and chassis of the production cars were made of ZAMAK (German: zink, aluminum, magnesium, and kupfer), also known as ZAMAC (U.S.: zinc, aluminum, magnesium, and copper). The New Jersey Zinc Company developed ZAMAC alloys in 1929.

Brass Olds 442; notice the brass roof and empty engine compartment

The interiors and windows on the brass cars were made using same technique as on the ZAMAC cars -- an aluminum injection mold. The windows were made of K-resin and the interiors usually of polypropylene material. These molds were also pantographed from larger models but were cut as a negative in the mold core so they could be used in an injection process. Once these brass cars were assembled they were hand painted to look just like the future production piece. Some brass cars had a tremendous amount of use, including catalog photos, TV commercials, and, of course, the all-important track testing. These particular promotional aspects needed to be completed well in advance of the cars' actual release.

Brass Mighty Maverick with brass revealed

Brass Mighty Maverick; notice the base with hardware screws

Even though a lot of time and money went into these brass cars, they typically had no purpose after the regular production of the casting started and were discarded.

At publication, there are twenty-five brass redline castings accounted for in private collections, two of which are in the Bruce Pascal collection.

Known Brass Cars To Date

Ambulance, Classic Cord,Evil Weevil, Funny Money, Grass Hopper, Ice T, Jet Threat, Mercedes C111, Mighty Maverick, Noodle Head, Olds 442, Paddy Wagon, Peeping Bomb, Power Pad, Sand Crab, Side Kick, Six Shooter, Short Order, Strip Teaser, Swinging Wing, What 4, Whip Creamer, Mongoose, Heavy Weight Cab & Chassis, Heavy Weight Racer Rig Trailer.

NOTE: The brass car manufacturing process was later used with the blackwall Demons, the Crack-Ups, and the Farbs.

5. LET THERE BE COLOR!
PAINT SAMPLES

Let's face it -- many have debated the reasons for the success of Hot Wheels. Was it the cars' super fast speed, creative names, "souped-up" styling, or perhaps the realistic colors? Other toy car companies were using relatively boring enamel paint, and along came Mattel with shiny metallic paint just like real muscle cars of the day.

Glowing red paint sample Hot Heap

In 1967, Albert Baginski was working in the preliminary design department when he came up with a revolutionary idea -- translucent paint on a polished car body would give the toy cars a modern, fresh look. Using the Ransburg Electrostatic System Paint Machine, many car bodies were test painted for the colors' look and quality. Hence, these surviving unassembled chassis are called "paint sample cars." Mattel was the first company to electrostatically charge toy cars for painting. Sample cars have been found for many different models, in many colors, but remain relatively hard to find, numbering in the hundreds in private collections.

Very rare magenta color Classic '32 Ford Vicky paint sample body

Albert described the magenta Classic '32 Ford Vicky (pictured above) as follows:

"The enclosed diecast body of a '32 Vicky 2 door Ford is from the first lot ever produced of that car model. The lot was bright barrel zinc plated and used for paint samples. They were electro statically painted individually on Ransburg equipment with translucent paint to give a "Candy Apple" look at my direction as an engineer working on getting the first ten Hot Wheels models in production for Mattel Toy Company. The "Candy Apple" concept was my idea rather than to use standard opaque paints, which were less attractive, in my opinion."

His technique took off! Mattel originally used Glidden paints for the first Hot Wheels cars and later switched to Bee Paints, ultimately purchasing the company.

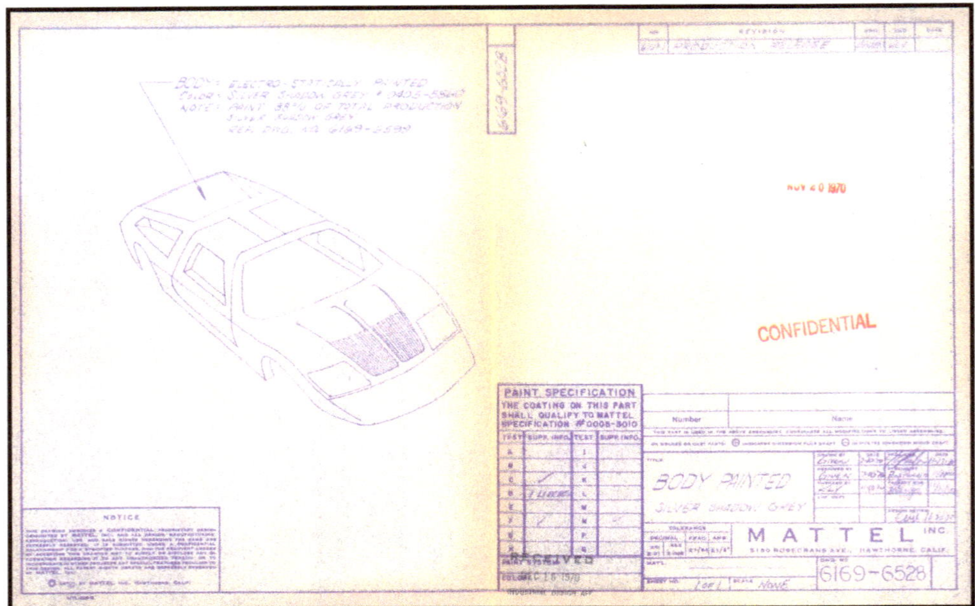

Confidential body paint order document for Mercedes-Benz C111 (1970)

Containers of Spectraflame paint (pink, olive-brown, yellow, and chocolate)

Gold painted body paint sample next to unpainted Custom Corvette

Very rare gold painted Boss Hoss spoiler prototype

CAR COLORS

HOT WHEELS COLOR CODE		COLOR	PAINT PART №	INK PART №
		CLEAR	0405 - 5610	
		BLACK-FLAT (AIR DRY)	0405 - 1310	
		SILVER	0405 - 1330	0405-5750
		TAIL LIGHT RED	0405 - 2700	0405-5690
		BLACK		0405-5700
		AMBER		0405-5840
03	1968	ORANGE	0405-5510	0405-5670
04		AQUA	0405-5520	0405-5660
06		VIOLET	0405-5530	0405-5680
07		LIME	0405-5540	0405-5620
09		GOLD	0405-5550	0405-5650
11		GREEN	0405-5570	0405-5710
13		BLACK-FLAT (BAKE)	0405-5580	
15		WHITE	0405-5590	
16		TOY RED	0405-5600	0405-5640
17	1969	FORD RED	0405-5720	
18		McLAREN ORANGE	0405-5730	
19		BRITISH RACING GREEN	0405-5740	
21		CERISE	0405-5770	
22		BROWN	0405-5780	
23		LIGHT BLUE	0405-5790	
24		BLACK-GLOSS	0405-5830	
25		DAY-GLO RED	0405-5850	
26	1968	BLUE	0405-5560	0405-5630
27	1969	OLIVE	0405-5760	
28	1969	SILVER SHADOW GREY	0405-5860	
29	1969	CHROME-PLATE	0005-5190	
31	1970	BLUE-OPAQUE (PADDY WAGON)	0405-5910	
32	1970	FERRARI RED	0405-5930	
33	1970	SNAKE YELLOW	0405 - 5960	
34	1970	MONGOOSE ORANGE	0405- 5950	

Hot Wheels color chart (1970) with color code numbers in right columns

Unpainted Custom Corvette raw body sample

Several colors were run on the car bodies and then presented to the marketing department. Once approved, those colors were used for production. The paint process is a prime example of how early test cars were vital to the development of Hot Wheels. Paint sample cars also provide many collectors with an opportunity to acquire a prototype, due to their affordability and quantity.

Brilliant red paint sample for the Silhouette

Spectraflame gold and aqua paint samples for the Classic '36 Ford Coupe

An internal 1970 memo showed the following colors for 1968-1970 cars: orange, aqua, violet, lime, gold, green, black-flat (bake), white, toy red, Ford red, Mclaren orange, British racing green, cerise, brown, light blue, black-gloss, Day-Glo red, blue, olive, Silver Shadow grey, chrome-plate, blue-opaque (Paddy Wagon), Ferrari red, snake yellow, and mongoose orange.

6. COOL PLASTIC
RESIN EPOXY MOLDED CARS

In the 1973 production year, Mattel began using resin epoxy castings instead of brass. The resin material was less expensive, lighter, and easier to work with, as it could be modified with greater ease than the brass. This also correlated well with Mattel's increasing use of plastic in the Hot Wheels car bodies post-1975, along with the introduction of the black walls (non-redline Hot Wheels) for mass production.

Resin 1/64 scale Second Wind (*left*) and assembled unpainted (*right*)

The resin epoxy model was pantographed from a hollow wood pattern and used to make a Silastic* mold. From that mold, usually twenty-four solid epoxy prototypes of the same model were cast in the 1/64 scale. These twenty-four prototypes had multiple purposes and were used for color samples, cosmetic variations, or as grid cars for tampo testing (see Chapter 7). Even though wheels and axles were typically placed on the resin cars, the one thing they were not used for was track accessory testing. The prototype car was usually too light to accurately gauge performance of the heavier production model.

Second Wind resin base below prototype assembled car

*Silastic™ is a trademark registered in 1948 by Dow Corning Corporation for flexible, inert silicone elastomer (plastic).

Resin casting of the Formula 5000 (*above*) and showing base and axles (*below*)

Of the twenty-four epoxy models, four would be cleaned up, painted yellow (for testing purposes), and sent to the equipment engineering department for tampo grid printing.

Hand painted resin casting of the Gremlin Grinder (*above* and *below*)

The twenty remaining epoxy test vehicles were painted in a regular production color, such as the blue on the Gremlin below, then printed with the final tampo graphic.

Plastic resin prototype Gremlin Grinder

Putting the graphics on numerous resin prototype cars allowed engineers to evaluate the quality and placement of the tampos over many samples, while also making sure the car color went well with the colorful tampo artwork.

Resin casting with Palm Beach tampo of the GMC Motor Home

7. THE LINES HAVE IT
THE GRID CARS

In 1972 Mattel began to realize it had a problem. The recession that was sweeping the country was also hurting the toy business, so Mattel began searching for ways to jumpstart sales and cut manufacturing costs. The planned switch to enamel paints in 1973 was to achieve both cost savings and compliance with new safety rules limiting heavy metals such as lead and arsenic in the Spectraflame paints. The problem was that the paint for the 1973 line of cars looked very much like the old Matchbox colors. Something needed to be done to the spice up the cars' plain-looking exteriors.

Classic Nomad grid car

Bob Rosas and George Soulakis, Mattel employees, heard about a new machine that created graphics that could be directly printed on plastic or metal surfaces. Called the pad printing machine, it produces what are known as tampos.

Demon, later to become Prowler grid car, (*left*) and production tampo car designed by Darryl Starbird (*right*)

Carabo grid car

George, excited about this invention, traveled to Germany to see the machine in use. The new process had the potential to be less expensive than applying stickers to the cars, and could really add excitement to the solid colors for Mattel's upcoming 1974 Hot Wheels.

After some financial analysis, the decision was made to buy the machines at $100,000 each, place them in Hong Kong, and add cool-looking graphics to most of the cars for 1974. Because the tampos were so colorful, this new Hot Wheels line would be called the Flying Colors.

Mattel also used the new machines for making the eyes on Barbie dolls. One problem arose. When printing on a flat surface, the tampos looked fine, but when printing on a curved surface, the graphics looked distorted. Mattel developed a system whereby they would apply a grid on a test car model to help position the graphics so the tampos would look even. Each grid was one-tenth of an inch square.

Grid patterns show the distortion that occurs as the tampo pad conforms to the vehicle body contours during printing. The grid also reveals the areas that will not tampo print due to body contours, recesses, and any other defects that may cause the pad not to come in contact with the vehicle body. Once the engineers see where the tampos will not work or look as good as they should, the industrial designer then draws tampo art details on a new sheet.

Next, a grid-printed car, showing the print distortion, and the hand-painted car, showing the final artwork, are sent out to a vendor for final artwork, including accommodation of distortion factors. From this final artwork a set of film positives are made and sent back to the equipment engineering department for making the tampo plates.

These grid cars allowed Mattel to conform the process to the contours of the cars. In many cases, existing castings from the Spectraflame years were used to save time and money, since making the tampos correctly for the grid cars was a time-consuming process, possibly explaining why only twelve new cars were made that year.

These grid cars actually had an extended life at Mattel: on many occasions, the same car model was reissued in a different color or with a new tampo in subsequent years. It is interesting to note that only one or two examples for each casting have ever been found. Consequently, grid cars are not only intriguing, but also very rare.

Baja Bruiser grid car (*above* and *below*)

Sweet 16 grid car (*above* and *below*)

Chaparral 2G, later to become Winnipeg, with grid pattern

Mercedes-Benz C111 white interior grid car (*left*), untampoed enamel (*center*) and tampoed production car (*right*)

Classic Nomad, later to become Alive '55, grid car (above); notice the grid pattern extended onto the wheels during the stamping process and even onto the windshield

Hand-painted tampo on side of Classic Nomad (one side only)

Hand-painted Formula 500

Mighty Maverick, later to become Street Snorter, grid car

Ice 'T' grid car; notice the grid pattern on interior seats

Rare untampoed blue Super Van

8. FIND THAT CAR!
CATALOG CARS

Timing is everything when it comes to meeting deadlines. This key phrase explains many of the mysteries surrounding the unique Hot Wheels catalog cars.

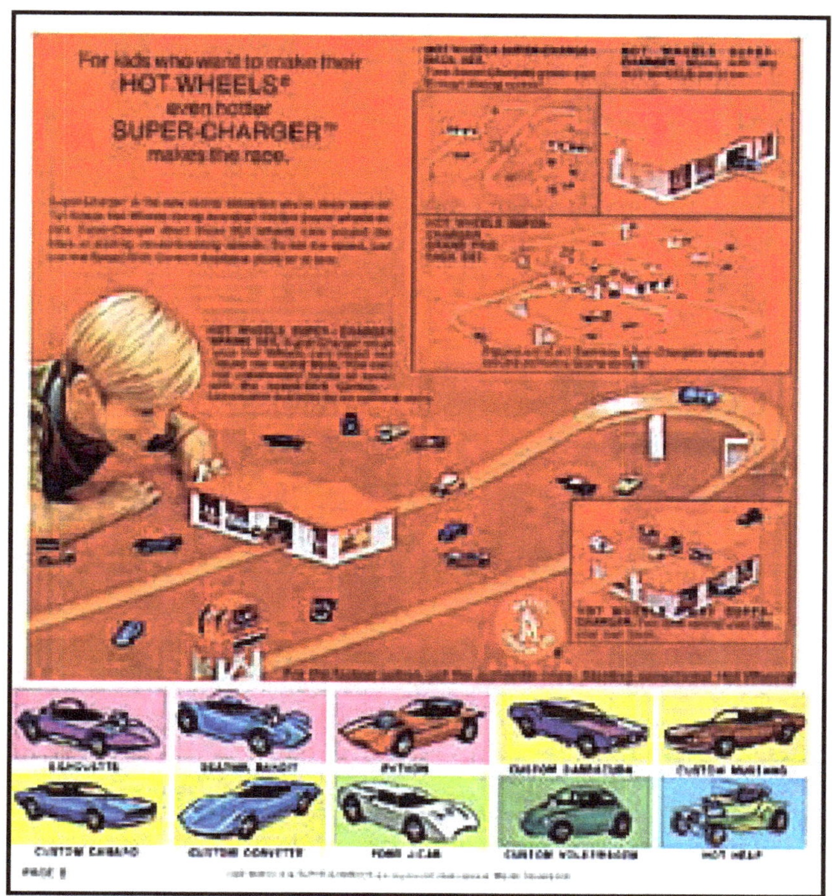

Because catalogs for the next year's Mattel products had to be prepared months in advance of a new Hot Wheels release date, many cars had to be photographed for the catalog before they were even made. Fortunately, Mattel had some tricks up its sleeve. If the car was not already produced, these tricks included:

1. Using a resin casting of the new product and hand painting it
2. Using the brass prototype that had already been made
3. Using chrome cars
4. Hand painting a previous model to look like the next generation soon-to-be-released (common on enamel painted cars after 1972).

The actual Indy Eagle car in front of the 1970 Hot Wheels catalog

Catalog brass Olds 442 with handmade base and *Olds 442* scratched into the bottom; the Olds 442 had one of the lowest production numbers

In 1968 Arvin Carlson ran the packaging department at Mattel and was responsible for hiring the artists and getting the cars photographed for catalogs. Jesse Cyr was one of the many artists employed there and remembers painting the tiny lettering and designs on Hot Wheels for the catalog photos. She said it could take over twenty hours to paint one tiny car!

The catalogs would typically showcase all the next year's models. The 1968 catalog pictured beautiful "Over Chrome Cars" (featured in Chapter 14) on the front cover.

Subsequent catalogs were filled with prototypes. Many collectors have searched their collections for the actual car used in a catalog or poster advertisement. Unfortunately, most collectors never find such castings since these were rare prototypes made exclusively for the photo shots.

Indy Eagle catalog car with no-redline front tire (*top*), alongside a rare green, white-interior Indy Eagle (*bottom*)

Indy Eagle catalog car with white interior and clear glass

9. CHANGE THAT NAME, AND *FAST*!
THE HOT WHEELS NAME GAME

The clever names Hot Wheels used for their toy cars were a major part of their commercial success. *Nitty Gritty Kitty* was much cooler to say and looked better on paper than *Mercury Cougar*! *Mod Quad* was a play on the name of the very popular show *Mod Squad,* in the '70s. Mustangs and Firebirds were treated to the prefix *Custom* to add that California vibe. Even the relatively boring school bus had to have a groovy and catchy name. You can't argue that *S'Cool Bus* was much cooler than *School Bus,* even though they basically sounded the same!

S'Cool Bus

Mattel was one of the first companies to use children to help name their toys. Alexandra Laird was responsible for coming up with many names and is credited with some of the most clever names in toy car history for Mattel. Alexandra would often suggest several names for one model, and then place the cars into plastic sandwich baggies labeled with the different names. Kids from age six to eleven years old would play in a room equipped with one-way glass and a microphone, and the Mattel researchers would observe which cars the kids played with.

The Drool Bus original hand drawing by Tom Daniel

For example, when the S' Cool Bus (1971 chopped School Bus, based on Tom Daniel's Funny Car Dragster) was being named, the baggies had several names written on them, including "Purple Pupil Hauler," "Drool Bus," "Cruel Bus," "No Principles Allowed," "Powered By Milk," "Impervious To Fuzz," "Sit-In-Stomper," "Pray for Summer," and of course, "S'Cool Bus." The original drawing for the School Bus, sketched by Tom Daniel in 1969, included the name "Drool Bus" on the side.

Two of the more famous name changes were the Cheetah (to Python) and the Mad Maverick (to Mighty Maverick). These names changed right after the initial production run because of possible licensing and legal issues.

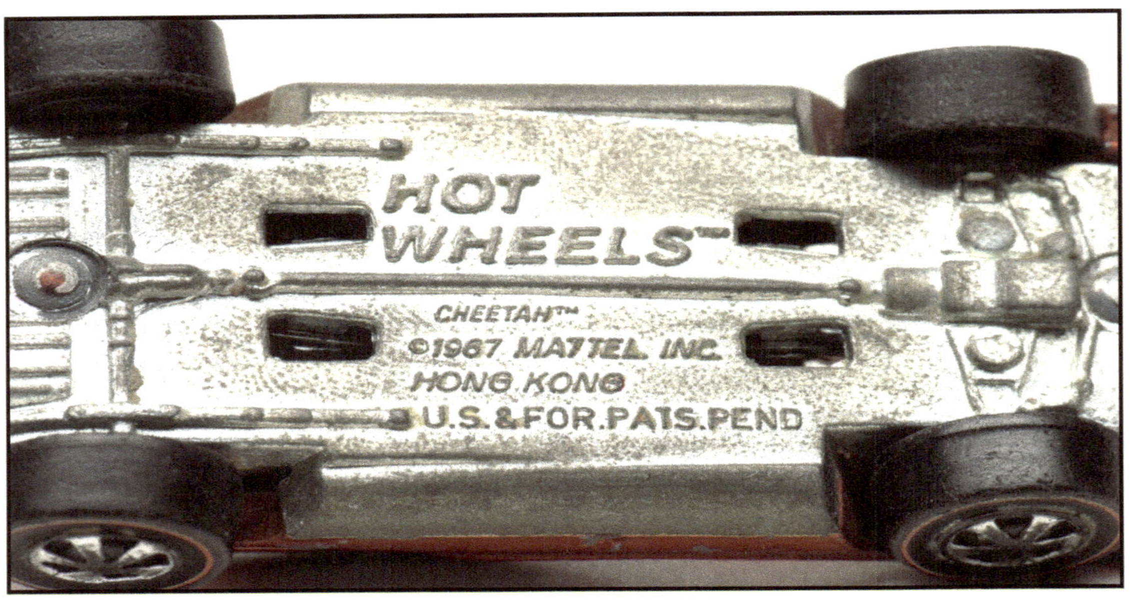

One very rare animal: the stamped Cheetah-base car (1967)

The problem with the Cheetah's name was that it belonged to and was trademarked by General Motors' executive Bill Thomas.

At the time, Thomas was building his own Corvette-powered Cobra Killer racecar, the Cheetah. Mattel wanted to avoid any legal issues so the name was changed. Less than six examples of Cheetah are known, including one very rare unpainted casting never assembled. It is interesting to note that on the backs of almost all the 1968 blister packs, the Python car is listed as Cheetah.

The Cheetah, based on Bill Cushenberry's Dream Car, designed for *Car Craft* magazine, was also a 1968 initial production year Hot Wheels

Red Cheetah prototype with edge wear

More commonly found in red, the example shown above was obtained by a man who had sent away for a cereal company promotion Mattel was doing at the time, and this was the car he received. Lucky guy!

Unassembled, unpainted prototype Mad Maverick

In 1968 Ford made a production car named Maverick, and Mattel wanted to make the car look better. Howard Rees, a Mattel designer, suggested adding a wing to its rear, spoiler stripes, and power bulges to the car to make it look faster. Using some alliteration, the name Mad Maverick sounded like a winner. But as soon as the car was made, Topper, a major competitor to Mattel and maker of Johnny Lightning Cars, came out with its Mad Maverick beating Mattel to the punch. So Mattel quickly changed its name for the car to Mighty Maverick. Amazingly, practically all of the Cheetah and Mad Maverick cars were destroyed. Only four examples of this car are known: one without paint with a clear plastic interior and wing; two in blue; and one in purple.

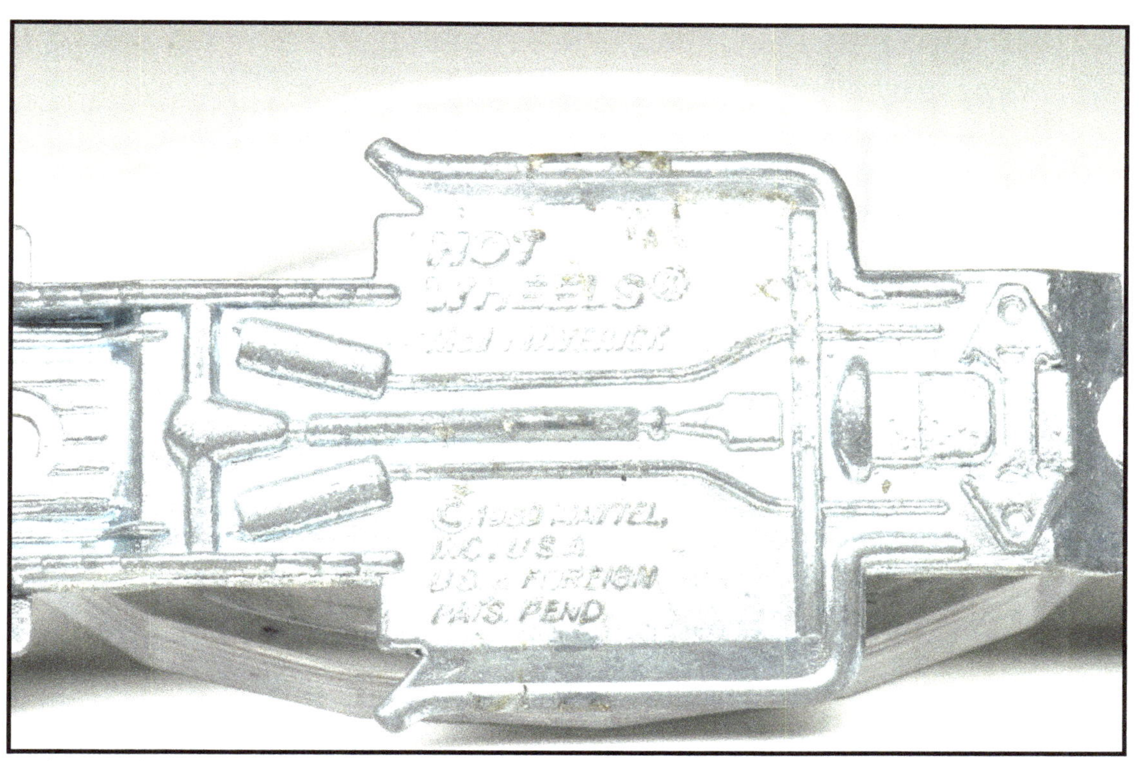

Pictured (*above*) is an unassembled base showing the name Mad Maverick

Unassembled parts of the Mad Maverick (*above*) and prototype Mad Mavericks with the original Ford Maverick wing plans (*below*)

10. LESS IS MORE (MORE OR LESS)
BLANK BASE CARS

Roger Newbold, a Mattel employee who drew technical plans for the Hot Wheels model makers, kept a log from his days at the factory. Roger's log outlined the production process and gave explanations as to why some Hot Wheels parts took longer to manufacture than others and why some cars had blank bases. A Hot Wheels toy car had an average of nine different parts that needed to come together on assembly day. The chassis, body, base, wheels, axles, hood, engine, clear glass, plastic interior, plastic seats, and sometimes even surf boards or stickers were all part of the final assembly. The base was the only part with imprinted information on the exterior of the car (car name, date, manufacturing country, and patent pending).

Blank base Mantises, nose to nose

In the Hot Wheels design game, the base stamping was usually the final step, to accommodate name selection delays or base design modifications. But in some cases, Mattel needed to put a car together before the final name was decided, leaving the base of the car essentially unfinished; for example, when an engineer needed to evaluate the fit, form, and function of the new model. This also allowed a car to be available for possible catalog pictures and advertising.

The Open Fire was designed by Mattel designer Alex Tam. The preliminary name for the casting was Allison Gremlin because the Gremlin casting displayed the enormous Super Charger Allison aircraft engine (yes, an airplane engine) in its extended engine bay. The base was extended to house the large engine, so the designers added a third axle in the front to balance out the design.

Courtesy of Wikimedia Commons (CC BY-SA 3.0)

Allison aircraft engine

Blank base Open Fire, based on the Allison aircraft engine, (*above*) and featured in its rare rose color (*below*)

No matter what the reason, a Hot Wheels blank base prototype is a rarity. Only a few blank base cars made it out of the factory and none were ever released to the public. Fewer than twenty blank base cars are known to exist, making them some of the hardest prototypes to find and rare examples of the Hot Wheels manufacturing process and timeline.

Blank base Mantis pair in purple (*left*) and orange (*right*)

Blank base Mercedes-Benz C111 (*above* and *below*) with painted base that also appeared on the regular production car

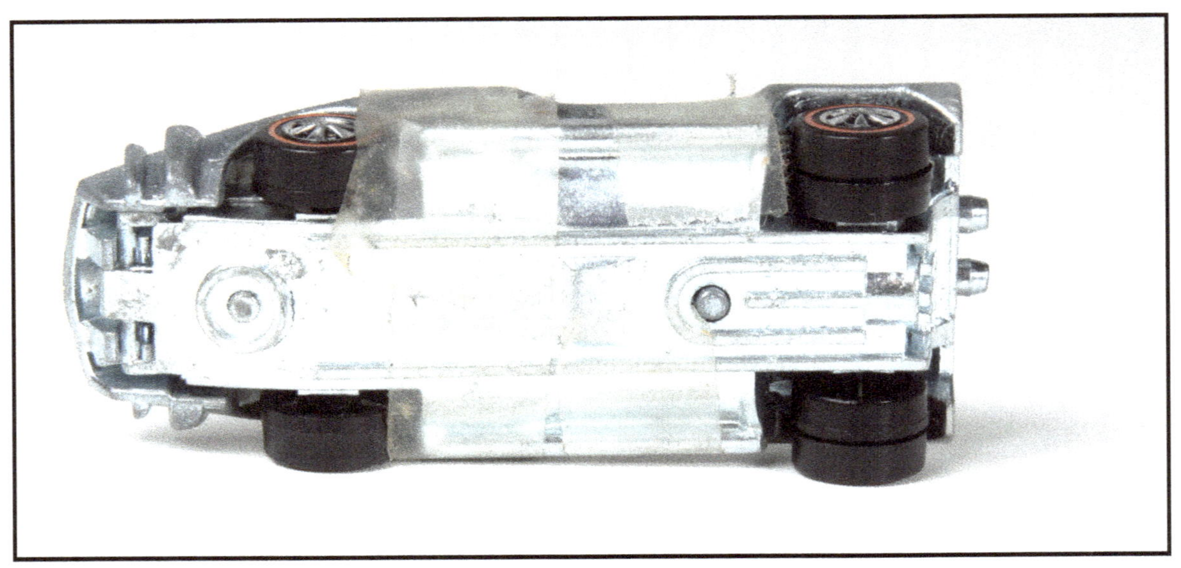

Prototype blank base Hairy Hauler (*above* and *below*), unassembled and unpainted

11. LOOKING UNDERNEATH
BASE VARIATIONS

One of the most common redline casting variations is the base variation. After production started, several Hot Wheels castings saw their bases redesigned but none as often as the Custom Camaro. The Custom Camaro base has been seen with openings shaped like rectangles, like kidney beans, with and without suspension tabs, and with a host of other variations, including even chromed.

Kidney bean Custom Camaro base (with kidney bean-shaped holes)

Early chromed base Camaro; note the Roman numeral XII on base

Classic '32 Ford Vicky with open suspension base and grill (early production; the normal production has closed suspension)

The Shelby Turbine, released for the 1969 Grand Prix Series, was based on a Mario Andretti turbine-powered racecar. After initial design, Mattel management realized it did not handle well with the Super Charger accessories because the car body was too thin to run through the Super Charger properly. So Mattel designed a plastic gas tank to fit underneath and on the sides of the car, drilled a hole in the bottom of the Shelby Turbine to affix the plastic part to, and started mass production. Only one example of the Shelby Turbine is known to exist without this hole.

Prototype Shelby Turbine no-hole base (*above*) production base (*below*)

The Seasider, a modified Chevy Fleetside carrying a boat, designed by Mattel designer Howard Rees for the 1970 production year, has one of the most commonly found early base variations. In the early production runs, most likely the final engineering pilot runs, the car was designed with a single exhaust pipe on each side of the base. Found mostly in orange and lime green colors, the single exhaust pipe was later changed to a dual exhaust, found in all the typical production run colors. No reason has ever been found for the difference in these two versions.

Single pipe prototype Seasider

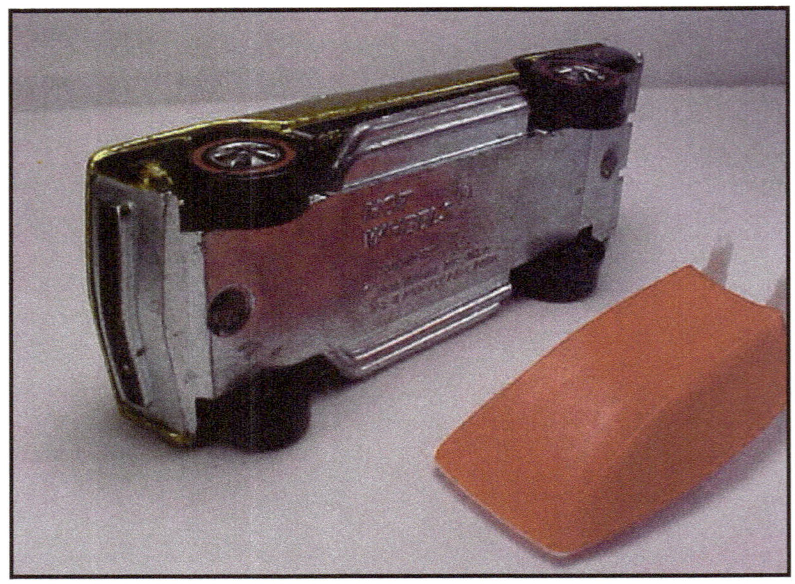

Regular production Seasider with double side pipes

Prototype Pit Crew Car (*above*) and (*below left*) alongside regular production Pit Crew Car (*below right*); notice the unpainted tools on the prototype

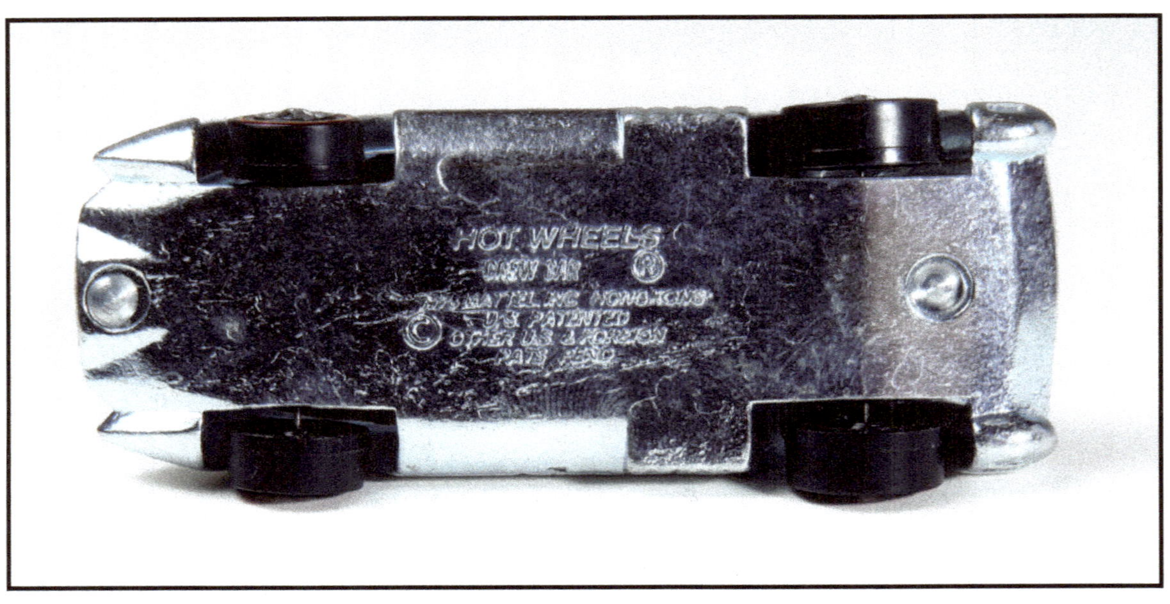

The Pit Crew Car, another concept car designed by Howard Rees and Larry Wood, had a base with an exposed suspension by each wheel. An early prototype (*above*) does not have these bars, one of only two examples known with this difference.

Mercedes-Benz C111 prototype base (*left*), and regular production base (*right*)
Note: The prototype base has no hole on the bottom

1st Shots
Rec'd 7-21-76
Acceptable

Two examples of a production base initially made of white plastic: the '57 Chevy (*previous page*) and the Fire Eater (*below*)

Fire Eater unpainted (*above* and *below*) with rare white plastic base

Z Whiz, unpainted, with first strike base, labeled June 25, 1976

Don "Snake" Prudhomme's Plymouth Barracuda unpainted first-strike base

Alive '55 unpainted and unassembled base (*above* and *below*); notice the unique two-color cap wheels and no redline on front wheel

12. HOT BODIES

BODY CASTING CHANGE VARIATIONS

Because the process of making the molds to cast the cars was one of the most time-consuming parts of the production timeline, very few Hot Wheels saw changes in their body castings after production started. Collectors love to find these variations, some of which are hard to find; others are easily spotted.

Major body variations were more commonly found in early production Hot Wheels (1968-1970). Production changes generally fall into three categories:

1. The original production molds broke and a new set was made with slight variations to the Hot Wheels car;
2. The designers suggested cosmetic improvements to make the car look better; and
3. Engineers designed improvements to better handle a Hot Wheels accessory — this could be the most dramatic change to the original casting.

Blue no-sunroof Custom Volkswagen (*right*) and orange production with sunroof (*left*); most of the no-sunroof cars were made in HK and sold in Europe

One of the more famous examples of a body change is the no-sunroof VW Bug made in the Hong Kong factory. This 1968 production casting of the popular 1967 Volkswagen Bug has been found predominately in blue and aqua, and less commonly in orange, red, green, green enamel, and copper colors.

The first Custom Volkswagens made in Hong Kong (HK) had a full roof, no side window glass, a unique interior featuring roll bars similar to a Baja Bug, and a higher rake to the body. Since this casting was made in Asia, the main distribution of these first-run cars was to Europe; most of them went to Germany and the U.K. on the Heisse Rader cards (German for *Hot Wheels*) or Brucia Pista (Italian for *Hot Wheels*). The California factory was actually behind the HK factory in making this casting. For some unusual reason, the molds for the HK cars originally came from the U.S., so the plot thickens as to when and why the cars were modified. The most common theory for the casting change is simple. The sunroof added a cool feature to the car's look and the little clear plastic sun roof could actually open and close and kids would love this feature. Adding the sunroof to the casting meant that the side glass and interior also had to be modified. It is thought that possibly within a day or so after production started on the HK cars it was halted because the Mattel designers preferred the sunroof model.

In 1974, Mattel reworked the U.S. casting of the Custom Volkswagen for the Flying Color cars, the colorful enamel painted cars with eye-catching tampos. Although the cars were also produced in Hong Kong without a sunroof, the design was actually closer to the original U.S. Custom Volkswagen with side window glass. It is interesting to note, however, that the parts of the Flying Colors Volkswagen are not interchangeable with the earlier no-sunroof Hong Kong Custom Volkswagens. That casting is highly sought-after by collectors because of the popularity of the VW Bug. With fewer than one hundred known to be in private collections, this rare variation is valuable.

Prototype antifreeze cut-fender Twin Mill

The 1969 Twin Mill was a revolutionary concept car designed by Mattel designer Ira Gilford, who had previously designed cars for General Motors. It featured two large exposed chrome engines behind the front wheels. The early prototype version has rear cut metal fenders whereas the regular production model has fender skirts covering the tops of the rear wheels. This is truly one of the more intriguing prototypes, because neither anyone who worked at Mattel nor any collector has offered a definitive reason as to why this design change was made.

Some speculate that the change was purely cosmetic; others, that the cut-fender version left the back wheels more susceptible to being bent when going through the Hot Wheels Super Charger machines and other track accessories.

Regular production hot pink Twin Mill (*left*) and two cut-fender Twin Mill examples, red (*top*) and antifreeze (*right*), designed by Ira Gilford

Fewer than ten examples of this prototype car have been found, including red and antifreeze (above), creamy pink, and a cool two-tone red-over-olive.

The Whip Creamer (pictured below) is another Hot Wheels car with body casting variations made after initial production molds. The 1970 concept car, designed by Paul Tam, was originally made without fins on its sides and with a larger back opening area by the turbine engine.

Hand carved fins on side of medium blue prototype Whip Creamer

The photo shows one of these rare prototypes having the fins hand carved into the sides to show Mattel management what the car would look like with these added. The other is a version with no fins at all. Each of these two examples shares other prototype characteristics, including non-production interiors and variations in the rear opening area, which is larger than in the final production model.

Variations of Whip Creamer prototypes: no-fins magenta (*bottom*), hand-carved fins medium blue (*center*), and light green with fins (*top*)

Prototype hand-carved fins on side of medium blue Whip Creamer (*left*) and regular production model (*right*) with changes to back area

T-4-2 with (*left*) and without (*right*) question mark on door

Question marks come to mind for a very rare casting body change recently discovered for the T-4-2 (above). This 1971 casting of a Model T cut in half and put together with two fronts going different directions was cleverly designed by Larry Wood, the best known of all Hot Wheels designers, previously an interior aircraft designer for Lockheed Martin. The initial name of the car was Which Way, later changed to T-4-2 for reasons unknown, but all of the regular production cars had a question mark cast on the doors.

Recently two blue cars were discovered without question marks. Why? Most likely the question mark was added by the designers after they created the car, to embellish it with a unique Hot Wheels flair.

Paddy Wagon (*above*), one of the most popular castings modeled after the full scale Paddy Wagon designed by Tom Daniel; prototype variations (*below*) with rare light blue and even rarer orange with orange roof (*center*)

Two very early drawings, dated December 25, 1970, of the original Rail Express, later called Special Delivery

13. OPTIONS ARE GOOD!
INTERIOR COLOR VARIATIONS

All first run Hot Wheels, whether made in the U.S. or Hong Kong factories, were tested at the factory in Hawthorne, California. These were called final engineering pilots, also known as FEPs. These cars were made in order to test the manufacturing process, examine the actual cars, allow the engineers to test them, and to time the production runs. When it came time to produce the interiors for these first-run cars, the employee would use plastic of whatever color happened to be in the injection mold machine at that time. As a result, the interior could end up green, light blue, black, or even a "Barbie doll" color. Whether one car was made or 1,000, these interior color variations are highly sought-after by collectors.

Several Hot Wheels cars are known for their scarce interior color variations, such as the Ford J Car with a white interior (one known), Rodger Dodgers with white interiors (few known), and the red Open Scoop Custom Mustang with a black interior (one known). The rarest of all interior colors is translucent plastic, with which only a few cars have been found.

Pictured is the only known translucent interior Mighty Maverick, designed by Howard Rees

Regular production Red Baron (*right*) and rare prototype with white interior (*left*), originally designed by Tom Daniel for Monogram

One of the most popular Hot Wheels designs is the Red Baron, which always came with a dark interior color. A scarce interior color variation is this white interior Red Baron (pictured above); less than ten are known to exist.

Collectors have found this slightly puzzling since the white interior looks better next to the red exterior than the regular production dark color and wonder why it was never used in production. This particular Red Baron car has a blank base and commands a very high value.

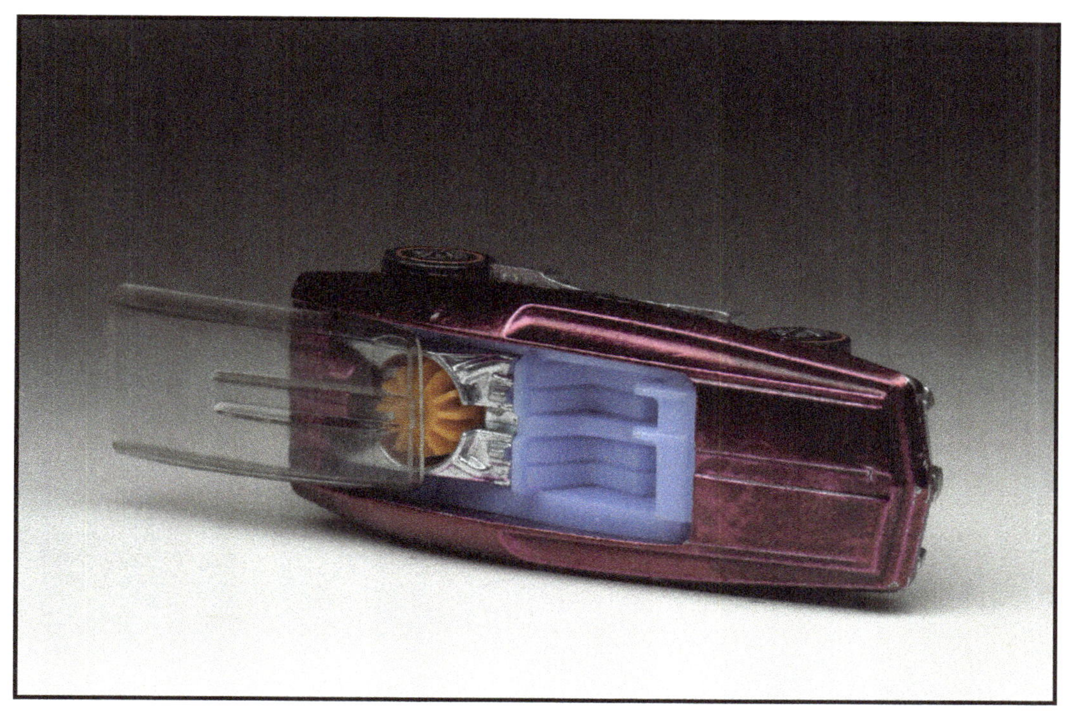

Super-rare blue interior Whip Creamer

Rare orange headlight with white interior Peepin' Bomb,
designed by Howard Rees

Prototype black interior Olds 442, designed by Larry Wood

White interior Ferrari 312P

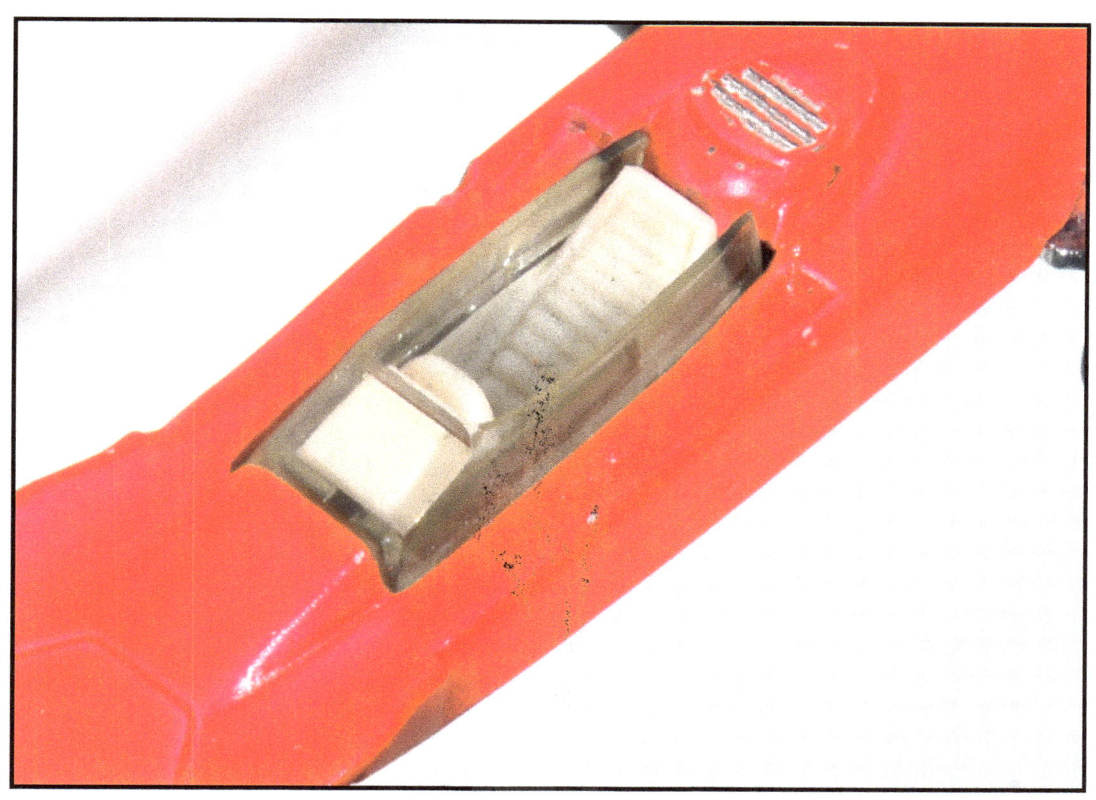

Orange with white interior and clear glass Lotus Turbine (*above* and *below*)

One-of-one double-shot red with black interior
Open Hood Scoop Custom Mustang

14. THE CROWN JEWELS OF THE HOBBY
1968 OVER CHROME CARS

There is some mystery surrounding the reasons the prettiest Hot Wheels cars were made, but many collectors agree that the Over Chrome cars stand out as the crown jewels of the hobby.

Over Chrome Custom Cougars

These cars look like they were chromed top and bottom and then painted, hence the descriptive name. It is speculated that these particular gems were created on or around the first day of actual production using a special two-step paint method that would differ from the regular production paint process for all subsequent Hot Wheels.

Paul Peterson assisted Harry Bradley in developing the colors for production Hot Wheels. During the initial test, painting was a two-stage process, using a pearl undercoat and then a paint overcoat to create a super-shiny "Over Chrome" paint. Quickly the R&D team realized that this two-stage process was expensive and time consuming, so they changed the paint process, tumbling the ZAMAK raw metal car bodies to polish them, then applying one coat of translucent paint. This became the regular process for millions of the cars made by Mattel. Since very few of these Over Chrome cars exist (in 2010, less than twenty were known), they are considered to be some of the most valuable Hot Wheels toy cars in the world; several of them were recently sold to private collectors for thousands of dollars each.

Thirty years after the first Hot Wheels rolled off the assembly line, Bruce Pascal discovered the existence of a large batch of these cars after receiving them from Arthur Stanley Woodward, a liaison engineer who worked at Mattel from 1965 to 1972. Stan, as he liked to be called, would typically keep the first products from any production run, whether it was a doll, a Mattel plastic rifle, or a Hot Wheels car, in case of production problems in Hong Kong. They could call him up day or night and he would always have an example of the toy with him.

Aqua Over Chrome Custom Barracuda with purple interior

The package contained Stan's collection of Hot Wheels, kept from his days at Mattel. Bruce purchased Stan's collection sight unseen and asked Stan to wrap each car individually in soft tissue paper so none would be chipped or damaged during shipment. Bruce received the highly anticipated package at work and called Curtis Paul, another avid Hot Wheels collector from the Washington, D.C. area, to come over and help unpack and witness the "event" on a brisk fall afternoon in 2001. As Bruce unwrapped the first car, they could not believe their eyes. Unveiled was one of the most beautiful antifreeze black-roofed Custom Camaros they had ever seen. The car literally shone like a Christmas ornament.

Over Chrome antifreeze Custom Camaro with green interior

The next car unwrapped was an orange Custom Cougar. This one also shone like a brilliant gem. As more cars were unwrapped the excitement grew, a gold Open Hood Scoop Custom Mustang, a gold Custom T-Bird, a purple Silhouette, an aqua Custom Barracuda with an outrageous purple interior, and more Custom Cougars and castings in different colors; all said and done, a total of eight "super" shiny Hot Wheels. Bruce turned to Curtis and stated that these cars were even better looking than any of the mint (unplayed with) cars that they had been accustomed to seeing.

Over Chrome blue black-roof Custom Camaro with light blue interior

Over Chrome antifreeze Silhouette

Bruce called Stan after the last car was unwrapped and asked him why some of the cars were so shiny and special looking. Stan said he remembers that the head guy in Hong Kong was told to make the first batch of Hot Wheels look like "Christmas ornaments" and to "make them look beautiful!" and didn't know much more than that. He did remember hearing that it took a long time to make the cars look this shiny and producing millions of cars in this manner just wasn't cost-effective. Interestingly, the chrome process that Mattel used on the first proof cars would not be repeated until a couple of years later, with the Club Kit cars. True gems of the Hot Wheels collecting world were discovered that autumn day!

"Birds of a feather stick together:" two Over Chrome aqua Custom T-Birds showing top and base

Fast forward to 2005, when a seller on eBay had a few other Over Chrome cars listed for auction. The seller had produced TV commercials for Mattel in the late 1960s. Luckily, he had kept an Over Chrome Custom T-Bird and a Custom Fleetside from 1968. After studying the earliest catalogs, it appears that these Over Chrome cars were the cars used in the photos. They had the same amazing shine in the eBay photos as they did in the original catalog photos. The sales price set a record and solidified the Over Chrome cars as the gems of Hot Wheels collecting.

Here's another great story to add to the Over Chrome mystique: in 1968, a young boy named Mark Fletcher and his two brothers came to the official Mattel Toy Store in California to buy some Hot Wheels with their family; unfortunately the store was closed due to an inventory check. His father, having promised the boys that they would get some Hot Wheels, decided to drive to Mattel's main headquarters a few blocks away, getting the address from the back of an empty Hot Wheel blister pack on the floor of the camper. Mark's father told the boys to wait in the camper and he walked into the office and explained his plight to the receptionist. The receptionist smiled and brought out a brand new track set to the camper where the boys were waiting. Realizing that she had only one toy for three boys, she kindly asked them to stay put for a few minutes.

Over Chrome gold Open Hood Scoop Custom Mustang

She then returned with a couple of loose Hot Wheels cars for Mark and his brothers. As it turns out, she had gone back into the building and grabbed two Hot Wheels cars from a back office. Mark and his brothers were lucky little boys that day because she handed them an Over Chrome orange Custom Cougar and a gold Open Hood Scoop Mustang. Mark, since he was the youngest boy, got the gold Mustang, which had a slight crack in the windshield. The better news is that Mark also got the orange Cougar soon afterwards, after he won a bet with his brother!

Over Chrome orange Custom Cougar

Whatever the reason these shiny little cars were made -- for catalog photos, TV commercials, or as some have suggested, as salesman's samples -- they rank as the crown jewels of Hot Wheels collecting.

All known original Over Chrome cars (excluding Club cars) and their colors:

- **Custom Camaro** - antifreeze and blue
- **Custom Cougar**- orange and blue
- **Custom Mustang** - gold and strawberry
- **Custom T-Bird** - aqua and gold
- **Custom Fleetside** – brown
- **Silhouette** - antifreeze and purple

15. CENTERPIECE OF THE HOBBY
THE REAR LOADER BEACH BOMB

In each collecting hobby, there is a highly sought-after piece that captures the attention and imagination of collectors. In the Hot Wheels world, it's the Rear Loader Beach Bomb. Much attention has been paid to this rare casting ever since the first hot pink version was discovered in 2000 and commanded a high price.

Since that moment in Hot Wheels collecting history, the focus on the Rear Loader Beach Bomb has been intense. Tens of thousands of collectors have dreamed of finding one for their own collection and scores of articles have been written on the piece, although at the time the pink version was discovered, little was known about the legendary casting. Like all prototypes, the question of scarcity is always a factor. Insiders have an idea as to the limited number in existence, and everyone else hopes that someday they will locate a forgotten one in a thrift store, pawn shop, or garage sale. Experts on the casting actually point out that there are not one, but two versions of the rarest Hot Wheels! There are other little known facts about how it was designed and how many of these "Holy Grails" were made. As research expanded, the behind-the-scenes details began to emerge; many of those details are revealed here for the first time. In order to best understand the existence of the Rear Loader Beach Bomb, we need to go back to the beginning of the project in the spring of 1969. Let's look at the Volkswagen Beach Bomb as it was first designed and follow its evolution.

Like other castings at Mattel, the original scale model was carved out of wood. The large-scale wooden model was shaped by Mattel employee Johnson Quarles. Johnson was the first person to complete Mattel's apprenticeship program in model making under the Division of Apprenticeship Standards, State of California. The Beach Bomb was his first carving, and it would prove to be his most significant. He would later carve the model for the Maserati Mistral.

The die-cast and injection mold tooling for the Rear Loader was created at the Neward Die & Manufacturing Company, in Upland, California. This company was hired by Mattel and charged with the responsibly for designing and building tools for most of the cars in the first several years of redlines. Plastic injection molding production facilities also existed at this location and were used to make various Hot Wheels plastic parts.

The first casting of this Beach Bomb was run as an engineering pilot, producing about 200 test-shot pieces, to demonstrate tool reliability and accommodate assembly fit tests. After a small number of Beach Bombs were assembled, concern was expressed that the Beach Bomb would not function with certain track accessories, namely the Super Charger. The Super Charger was an accessory that could make the car move fast over the track using spinning wheels rotating very fast that would propel the car forward. Mattel employee Alan Nash filmed the Beach Bomb as it powered through the Super Charger, and then ran the film back in slow motion to study the physical dynamics of the car as it flew erratically out of the wheelhouse. It was the tallest, narrowest, and most top-heavy Hot Wheels car ever assembled, and because of this, it had the highest center of gravity. These attributes created instability on the track sets, compromising the car's play value.

Several of the engineers involved were asked to take samples home and see if their children had any problems with this known design flaw. While the children all found the car to be very cool aesthetically, they were disappointed by the fact that the Beach Bomb would not function properly with the Super Charger, and that it rolled off of any curve it encountered.

The tooling was complete and functional. They had a new casting that was great-looking. Marketing was already photographing the new car for sales and promotional materials, but the problem of the new casting's incompatibility with many track accessories still loomed, and Mattel engineers went into salvage mode. A number of proposed changes to the casting were considered; every engineer had an idea on the table. Drawings were modified with over 150 changes to the die cast and injection mold tooling. The goal was clear: Lower the center of gravity and widen the wheelbase. The mission was tricky, however, because changes had to conform to the tooling that already existed. This new twist to the project was not a redo, but rather a touch-up.

Beach Bomb base (transitional base)

Several key structural changes made the car more stable on the track sets:

- The sunroof was expanded in size by three hundred percent, as the loss of metal on the roof made the car less top-heavy;

- The overall height of the car was reduced by about one-eighth inch, bringing the center of gravity down closer to the track;
- A counterweight was added to the chassis to lower the center of gravity (which no other casting before or since has featured!); and
- Rear quarter panels were pushed out about one-fourth inch in total; the new boxy shape of the rear was cleverly utilized as a pocket system for the surfboards, which were originally designed to be inserted into the rear window.

Once the new Side Loader casting modifications were implemented in the production tooling, the small numbers of Rear Loader Beach Bomb castings were set aside and all but forgotten. Many of them were still in the hands of the engineers, and in some cases, in the toy boxes of the engineers' children who had been involved in the initial testing.

Once the first Rear Loader was discovered by collectors in 1980, it quickly became the holy grail of Hot Wheels collecting. Soon others were found, and by the mid-1990s, over thirty were held in private collections. Meanwhile, others rested in hidden old collections and junk boxes, just waiting to be discovered. By now, forty-one are known to have surfaced (2010 estimate). One can only speculate how many more survived and where they will be found.

Though there are ten different colors of the Rear Loaders known, including the unpainted ZAMAC, the most sought-after color is the hot pink. There have been only two hot pink Rear Loaders ever discovered, and they have vastly different bases.

Before acquiring the first Pink Beach Bomb (RLBB1), Bruce conducted a tremendous amount of research to determine its authenticity and validate its provenance. He went so far as to locate and contact the original owner of the RLBB1 and has since received letters of authenticity from the original owner documenting the car's history and origin.

After interviews and meetings with people involved in the design of the RLBB, Bruce was satisfied with the car's authenticity. He went ahead and purchased the first pink RLBB, paying a record amount. The actual purchase price has never been disclosed; however, at the time, anyone willing to spend $72,000 could have become the owner.

Since purchasing the hot pink RLBB1, Bruce has continued to research the history of the casting. He has been successful in contacting former employees, looking up retirement rosters, researching older Mattel newsletters, and using a referral approach to track down anyone who could add information to this unique casting.

RLBB1 is unique in a number of ways. The body is from a Rear Loader Beach Bomb, and all the other components are from a Side Loader Beach Bomb. The chassis and the body are mated under unusual tension. The rear post was spun first, then the front. With the rear fixed in position, the chassis would have to be pressed down to mate with the body properly. In order to strike the posts and rivet the chassis onto the body, the car would have to be held steady while the spinning striker put considerable pressure on the chassis. This pressure would enable the post to protrude from the hole in the chassis.

Once the front post was exposed, it would be struck. The first attempt at this failed, and rendered a circular blemish on the underside of the car where the striker missed the front post.

In Bruce's constant search for more information about his hot pink RLBB1, he made contact with Peter White, a retired Mattel employee living in southern California. Peter was a former liaison engineer involved in production and research and development. He told Bruce over the phone that he had a collection of cars from the years he worked at Mattel and one of them was a Beach Bomb. After a few questions about the cars, Bruce determined that several of the cars were pre-production or prototype cars and Bruce also determined that the Beach Bomb was a Rear Loader Beach Bomb.

White also told Bruce that the Beach Bomb was pink. Bruce figured it must be rose or magenta or some other color since there was only one pink Rear Loader known and he had it. Bruce purchased the collection and when the package arrived, he was in utter disbelief as he opened it to reveal another hot pink Beach Bomb! (RLBB2) Both cars came from liaison engineers at Mattel, who typically would have been allowed to take the toy cars home with them.

Chris Marshall, who had sold RLBB1 to Bruce, had originally purchased RLBB1 from Jacobus Van Nimwegen, another former liaison engineer working with Mattel on the project in 1969.

Since purchasing the original RLBB1 from Chris Marshall, Bruce has always believed that there must be more Rear Loader Beach Bombs out there. The Letter of Authenticity sent by Peter White, the owner of the second pink Beach Bomb, disclosed that there were two hundred engineering pilots produced. It became clear that the possibility of additional examples certainly exists.

Unpainted prototype Rear Load Beach Bomb base with no interior

In his travels, Bruce found another former Mattel employee who had some fascinating documentation, and another Rear Loader Beach Bomb. Roger Newbold maintained a log of production dates associated with the Beach Bomb project. Now we have absolute information regarding the run dates of each individual component of the Beach Bomb. Roger's notes explained why some

Rear Loaders exist without interiors: the die-cast parts were available for assembly before the plastic injection-molded parts were complete. So some Rear Loader Beach Bombs were assembled with only the body and chassis.

Roger's Rear Loader Beach Bomb had never been painted. Bruce was fortunate enough to have to opportunity to acquire this piece for his collection.

Rare double paint shot purple prototype Rear Loader Beach Bomb with no interior

Prototype Side Load Beach Bomb (*left*) & RLBB1 (*right*)

The RLBB1 has a transition base, which is the actual production-model base (wider), and the RLBB body (skinnier). The other pink Beach Bomb (RLBB2) has the correct non-production base and body, as well as other characteristics of RLBB: clear windshield glass, rear-loader interior slots for the surfboards, smaller sunroof, and other casting characteristics seen in all the other RLBBs.

The first casting had a short rear engine cover; later castings went to a long rear engine cover. This change was made to provide a physical stop on the chassis for the engine to rest against during assembly. Before the hatch was extended, the assembly process hyper-inserted the chassis into the body, causing cosmetic and structural disfigurement of the rear bumper. Quite possibly, the pink Rear Loader Beach Bomb with the wider transitional base may be one of the, if not *the,* last assembled Rear Loaders. This casting also has the longer rear engine cover, as do all of the second-run Rear Loaders.

Numbers and known colors of Rear Loader Beach Bombs

Rear Loader Type A with short rear engine cover (1st run)

3 – ZAMAC

3 – Anti-freeze

1 – Light blue

2 - Gold

7 - Green

7 – Red

23 Type A

Rear Loader Type B with long rear engine cover (2nd run)

1 –ZAMAC

3 – Dark blue

1 – Light blue

3 – Purple

1 – Dark purple

1 – Rose

1 – Rose with black roof

1 – Red enamel (shortened body and chassis)

1 – Pink

1 – Pink with transitional wider base

14 Type B

Transition Loader Type C (rear and side loader surfboards) and short rear engine cover

2 - ZAMAC

1 - Antifreeze

1 – Unknown color, privately held overseas

4 Total Type C

41 – Grand Total

REAR LOAD BEACH BOMB Time Line

11 February, 1969:

Body: Mattel date the body drawings were to be completed.

14 February, 1969:

Chassis: Mattel date the chassis drawings were to be completed

23 February, 1969:

Interior: Mattel date the interior drawings were to be completed

25 February, 1969:

Window: Mattel date the window drawings were to be completed

May 1969:

All parts: Newards required at least twelve weeks to return a completed car.

October-November 1969:

Car Mattel: Type 2 Rear Loader Beach Bomb car with prototype Side Loader Beach Bomb base shows up

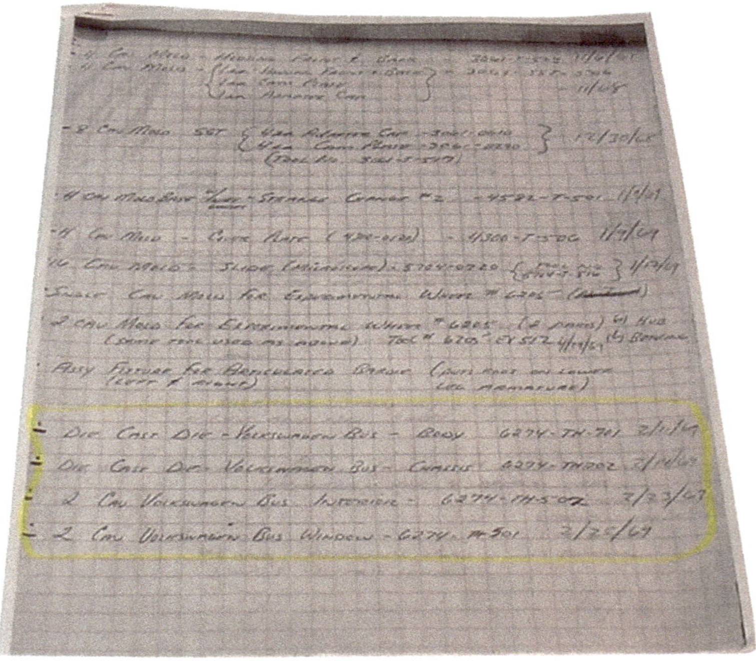

1 Die Cast Die - Volkswagen Bus - Body 6274-TH-701 2/11/69
1 Die Cast Die - Volkswagen Bus - Chassis 6274-TH-702 2/14/69
2 Cav Volkswagen Bus Interior - 6274-TH-502 2/23/69
2 Cav Volkswagen Bus Window - 6274-TH-501 2/25/69

Mattel employee personal log (3-25-1969)

16. SUMMARY

Over the past forty-plus years, Hot Wheels have become a big part of many childhood memories. Seeing a little shiny car buzzing down the orange Hot Wheels track is exciting! But, just like any great idea, it must start from somewhere or with somebody.

At first, it may just be a thought or a concept that needs to be put on paper (drawn) and/or eventually made into a tangible object (prototype). It is these very first attempts at making the tangible objects that so fascinate the collector. Going from point A to point Z and seeing the evolution of the prototype design is truly an amazing journey.

Going from the very first little prototype car that rolled off Elliot Handler's desk to the 'One Billionth' Hot Wheels has impacted die-cast car interest since the first day they 'hit' the shelves. Luckily for collectors, people like Bruce Pascal, through drive and determination, have provided many of the missing links to the history of the Hot Wheels story.

Bruce Pascal's journey to validate one of the most famous prototype Hot Wheels, the Rear Load Beach Bomb, has led to one of the most extensive prototype die-cast car collections seen in the hobby to date.

Ironically, what has made many of these initial toy car designs so valuable is that most of them were thrown away or trashed. But as we have discovered, some of these rare cars were saved by the original employees and many have made their way into Hot Wheels collectors' and enthusiasts' hands to be enjoyed and cherished for years to come. And with each discovery there is hope that more little gems are still out there, waiting for their story to be told and so they may take their rightful place in the Hot Wheels history books.

Elliot Handler with Bruce Pascal, Los Angeles (2002)

Elliot and Ruth Handler playing with Hot Wheels (1969)

Bruce Pascal and the Pink Rear Loader Beach Bomb (2000)

APPENDIX 1:
SHOWCASE OF PROTOTYPES

Mighty Maverick grid car

Sweet 16 grid car

Baja Bruiser grid car

Corvette paint samples

Chaparral grid car

Mercedes Benz C-III grid car

Ice 'T' grid car

Alive '55 grid car

Steam Roller grid car

Custom Volkswagen Beetle grid car

Antifreeze The Demon grid car

Aqua & Antifreeze Custom VW Bug grid cars

Aqua Turbofire black interior

Rose Open Fire blank base

Breakaway Bucket no tampo, raw ZAMACbase

Chrome Shelby turbine Dinner Car

Cut fender Twin Mill two tone color

Burnt orange Mantis blank base

Red enamel Fire Chief

Unpainted Police Cruiser

Harry Hauler
with "Little Man" driver

Tow Truck
clear window, no paint

Red Baron
white interior, blank base

Seasider
clear interior, single pipe on base

Nitty Gritty Kitty
no front grill paint

Brass Olds 442
catalog car

Brass Mighty Maverick
catalog car

Spectraflame Blue Paddy Wagon

Red Open Hood Scoop Custom Mustang (black interior, only one known)

Top Eliminator
capped wheels

Whip Creamer
clear interior,
casting difference in rear

Coral Enamel Swingin' Wing
similar to catalog car

Gold Enamel Classic '57 Bird
similar to catalog car

Blue Mad Maverick
one of three known

Mighty Maverick
clear plastic interior and wing

Red enamel Fire Chief

Matchbox/Hot Wheels hybrid
one of earliest prototypes known

Custom Camaro painted over
raw casting
no pat. pending on base

Very early Number 2 Camaro
(not yet called "Custom")

Very early Custom Camaro
painted over ZAMAC

Matchbox/Hot Wheels hybrid one of earliest prototypes known

Green Bye-Focal no injectors, clear glass

Seasider single exhaust pipe and all-orange boat

Red Cheetah

Odd Job hand-painted

Sizzler prototype wheels

Sizzler experimental slot-car base

Orange Ford Mark IV

Steerable yellow Ford Monte Carlo prototype

Orange steerable Super Van prototype

Black enamel Mercedes C111 Steerableing ability

Steerable lime Continental Mark III

Brown Classic '31 Woody

Lime Custom Cougar painted nose cone

Aqua King Kuda Hong Kong, clear glass

Red Olds 442 black interior

Orange Classic '32 Ford Vicky open suspension

Blue Classic '32 Ford Vicky open suspension

Antifreeze Classic '32 Ford Vicky open suspension

Watermelon Classic '32 Ford Vicky

Unassembled aqua
Classic '32 Ford Vicky

Shelby Turbine
featured in 1970 catalog

Indy Eagle
clear glass, white interior,
featured in 1970 catalog

Red test run Tri Baby
no/white interiors

Red Ferrari 312P
white interior

Blue Shelby Turbine
white interior, no hole in
base

Orange enamel Lotus
Turbine
white interior, clear glass

Orange Custom Fleetside
painted base

Olive Brabham Repco F1
white interior, clear glass

Blue Indy Eagle
white interior, clear glass

Spectraflame Olive Indy
Eagle
white interior, clear glass

Red Indy Eagle
black base

Magenta Python
(misfit windows - USA)

Purple Whip Creamer
(white interior)

Orange Peepin' Bomb
orange headlights

Purple Peepin' Bomb
orange headlights

Light green The Hood
black top

Antifreeze Custom
Camaro
early kidney-bean base

Magenta Mercedes Benz
C-111
blank base

Resin Gremlin Grinder

Purple Mantis
blank base

Apple Green Strip Teaser
blank base

Unpainted Porsche
Carrera
blank base

Antifreeze Cut Fender
Twin Mill

White Pit Crew Car
no suspension on base

White ladder Fire Engine

Resin A-OK

Blue Super Van
with Yamaha tampo,
only one known

Aqua Light-My-Firebird
Hong Kong, clear glass

Blue Custom Volkswagen
no sunroof

Gold Mercedes-Benz
280SL
only one known

Chrome Sir Rodney
Roadster

Heavy Chevy
not over chrome, only two
known

Clear production-testing
Sizzler

Clear Prototype Study
Car

Lincoln Continental
Mark III Flip Out car

Flip Out prototype

Noise-Making
Continental Mark III

Purple Ford J-Car
white interior, only one
known

White Baja Bruiser
hand-painted

Dark Blue Alive '55
tampo on driver side only

Mercedes-Benz C111
prototype tampo

Mercedes-Benz C111
no tampo

White Custom Camaro

Lincoln Continental
dark interior

Blue Rodger Dodger

Plum Rodger Dodger
white interior

Hi Raker Rodger Dodger
prototype

Reverser Sizzler prototype

1975 Winter Ball
Chevy Manza

1976 Gold Porsche
Salesman's Award

1975 Toy Fair Van

Black enamel Chapparal

Black enamel Ford Mark IV

Black enamel Hot Heap

Black-fendered Police Cruiser

Black enamel Torero

Black enamel Turbofire

Unpainted Cockney Cab

Unpainted Zinc-plated Side-Loading Beach Bomb

Unpainted, unassembled
Mod Squad
white interior

Unpainted, unassembled
Porsche 917

Unpainted, unassembled
Grass Hopper

Unpainted Hiway Robber
white interior

Unpainted Twin Mill

Unpainted Torero

Unpainted T-Bird
with doorlines

Unpainted Splittin' Image

Unpainted Neet Streeter

Unpainted Custom T-Bird
first one produced in U.S.

Unpainted Custom
Camaro

Unpainted Classic
Nomad
prototype wheels

Unpainted Classic '36 Ford coupe

First Custom Camaro base assembled in U.S.

Unpainted Continental Mark III black interior

Unpainted, unassembled Bug Eye

Raw casting Odd Rod black cabin

Unpainted Hiway Robber white interior, numbered

Raw ZAMAC Z-Whiz

Raw ZAMAC GMC Motor Home

Raw ZAMAC '31 Doozie

Raw ZAMAC '57 Chevy

Raw ZAMAC '57 Chevy chassis

Raw ZAMAC Fire-Eater

Raw ZAMAC Haulin' Horses

Raw ZAMAC Letter Getter

Raw ZAMAC Second Wind

Raw ZAMAC Show Hoss

Heavyweight Ambulance with clear glass

Red Shelby Turbine with plastic gas tanks

Street Rodder no tampo

Street Rodder hand-painted resin

Unassembled Classic Nomad prototype wheels

Unassembled light blue Custom T-Bird

Magenta Fuel Tanker

Yellow S'Cool Bus

Chrome '36 Ford Coupe paint test

Gold '36 Ford Coupe paint test

Aqua '36 Ford Coupe paint test

Red Hot Heap paint test

Red Silhouette
paint test

Magenta Classic '32 Ford
Vicky
paint test

Gold Torero
paint test

Gold Custom
Volkswagen Bug
paint test

Gold Custom Eldorado
paint test

Orange/red enamel
Charger

Chromed (vulcanized)
Mustang Stocker
only one seen with this
tampo

Enamel Power Pad

Myles Ahead
resin Farb prototype

Unpainted Farb

Resin Farb

MegaForce motorcycle
prototype
never released

Purple Peepin' Bomb
white interior

Torino Stocker
with screwed base

Corvette Stingray
with screwed base

Spectraflame blue Buzz-
Off

Pink Show Hoss
raw base,
redlines blackened over

Pink Show Hoss blank top

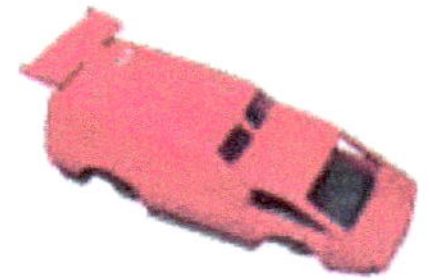

Pink Spoiler Sport
unassembled raw casting

Pink Haulin' Horses
only known loose
example

Resin GMC Motor Home

Resin Porsche Carrera

Team Trailer
green-tinted rear windows

Zowee
never issued

Zowee Goin' Fishing non-production color

Zowee Light My Fire prototype

Zowee Fire Truck prototype

Zowee Home Sweet Home prototype

Zowee Numb Skull prototype

Fire Engine Heavyweights white ladder, enamel cab

Unidentified prototype

Smoke window Maserati Mistral

APPENDIX 2:
SHOWCASE OF ORIGINAL DOCUMENTS AND DRAWINGS

Harry Bentley Bradley
Car Design Car Illustration

HARRY BENTLEY BRADLEY'S
HOT WHEELS
ARCHIVES

JANUARY 03

Harry Bradley's car illustrations cover letter, January 2003, to Bruce Pascal

Harry Bentley Bradley
Car Design Car Illustration

JANUARY 03

12 LINE SKETCHES

THESE ARE 'B' SHEET SKETCHES I DID AT MATTEL QUITE EARLY IN 1967... THE CUSTOM FLEETSIDE PIECE IS DATED 4-3-67. IN NO PARTICULAR ORDER:

1. CAMARO
2. FLEETSIDE
3. DEORA
4. SILHOUETTE
5. COUGAR (1 of 2)
6. COUGAR (2 of 2)
7. BARRACUDA
8. PYTHON/CHEETAH
9. FORD J CAR
10. BEATNIK BANDIT
11. FIREBIRD
12. AVANTI

EXCEPT FOR THE FLEETSIDE PIECE WHICH HAS BEEN DONE IN INK, THESE SKETCHES ARE PRELIMINARY OR UNDERLAY PIECES. I WOULD HAVE LIKELY DONE COLOR RENDERINGS FROM THESE. THE RENDERINGS WOULD HAVE BEEN SHOWN TO MANAGEMENT BY ME IN A PRESENTATION MEETING SO THEY COULD EVALUATE

Harry Bradley's original letter to Bruce Pascal on the sale of the first ever Hot Wheels B sheet sketches

12 LINE SKETCHES pg 2

EACH CAR & GET AN OVER-VIEW of THE ENTIRE LINE UP.

IT'S POSSIBLE THE 11 PENCIL SKETCHES WERE DONE MUCH EARLIER THAN THE INK PIECE BECAUSE THE SELECTION of CARS HAD PRETTY WELL TAKEN SHAPE BY EARLY SPRING, 1967. MANAGEMENT WANTED CORPORATE DIVERSITY — SOME GM CARS, SOME FORD CARS & SOME CHRYSLER CARS. NO AMERICAN MOTORS CARS, THOUGH — AMC WAS FAILING BADLY AT THAT TIME & WE BELIEVED THERE WOULDN'T BE ANY INTEREST IN THEIR PRODUCT LINE. WE ALSO BELIEVED WE SHOULD HAVE SPORTY STUFF AS WELL AS LUXURY CHOICES: MUSTANGS & T-BIRDS (BIG LUXURY CARS BY THE MID-60s) AND CAMAROS ALONG WITH ELDORADOS. I INTRODUCED MATTEL TO HOT RODS & CUSTOM BUILT SHOW CARS WHICH ADDED ANOTHER LAYER of INTEREST TO THE MIX.

AMONG THESE SKETCHES, 5 CARS ARE MISSING THAT WERE, of COURSE, INCLUDED IN THE LINE

1. MUSTANG
2. ELDORADO
3. CORVETTE
4. HOT HEAP
5. VW BEETLE

THESE SKETCHES WERE PROBABLY DESTROYED... OR LOST.

THE BARRACUDA SKETCH HAS LISTS of OTHER POSSIBLE CARS I WAS CONSIDERING OR ASKED TO CONSIDER... I NEVER LIKED MILITARY VEHICLES MUCH, SO THE LATTER WAS LIKELY THE

Harry Bradley's letter, page 2

12 LINE SKETCHES pg 3

CASE:

I WAS PUSHING FOR THE AVANTI -- IT WAS A REAL DESIGNERS' CAR. BUT MATTEL THOUGHT IT WAS NOT AT ALL WELL KNOWN & THEY WANTED VERY POPULAR OR AT LEAST VERY EXCITING CARS IN THE LINE.

WHY THE 2 COUGAR SKETCHES? THE 1ST ONE HAS AN EXTREME PERSPECTIVE -- CAR DESIGNERS IN THE '60s LIKED THIS "FORCED" PERSPECTIVE TECHNIQUE BECAUSE IT MADE CARS LOOK SO WIDE, AGGRESSIVE & STYLISH... BUT, MATTEL, NOT AT ALL USED TO SUCH BOLD DISTORTION IN THEIR DESIGN WORK, ASKED ME TO MAKE MY RENDERINGS MORE REALISTIC. I THEREFORE THINK THE ONE COUGAR SKETCH & EVEN THE CAMARO SKETCH PRE-DATE THE OTHERS BY POSSIBLY A MONTH OR SO. THEY MAY EVEN BE LATE 1966!

WHATEVER THEIR DATE, THEY ARE MOST CERTAINLY THE EARLIEST HOT WHEELS DESIGN WORK THAT WE HAVE... THEY COULD EVEN BE EARLIER THAN THE ACTUAL NAME HOT WHEELS.

Harry Bentley Bradley

Harry Bradley's letter, page 3

Product Design Model Milestone Summary

1) Required input

R&D Release Date:

This date will influence all milestones to be scheduled on this outline and should be established when a toy number is assigned by product planning.

"B" Sheet. Shows basic concept of toy and is a guide to finalizing appearance drawing for models to be built.

3 Dimensional or Assembly drawing. Appearance models can not be built until these drawings are made. The project will make better progress if time is taken at this point to make a design layout (velum) or an assembly drawing showing all interfacing parts. Part drawings to be lifted off this valuable original design drawing.

Design Approval. Project manager should approve this drawing in the space provided before a lot of model activity takes place.

Parts list. Usually firmed up late in the design phase but is very helpful in listing long lead time tool items so temporary alum. molds of key parts can be scheduled. Any list is helpful in making out the project budget.

Total Model Shop Hours. Show hours taken from approved R&D project budget.

Supervisor Assigned. To show Model Maker supervisor responsible for all model making and master pattern making on each project.

2) Mechanism

On mechanical toys, build

a) 2D side plate model-2,5, or 10 x size; profile parts or templates mounted on ply wood with pins and rubber bands.

b) 3D Bread Board Model. All functional parts constructd and housed between 2 plates of lucite (¼")

3) Acetate appearance model

A solid model cut, carved and machined from colored celuloso acetate. An excellent medium for small detailed objects, i.e. Skies, axe,

Product design model milestone summary #1

11) Tooling requirements.

If the product shape cannot be defined easily by dimensional prints an upshrink pattern is usually required with parting line (follow board) definition. Tool engineering should be consulted before pattern construction.

12) a) Life test parts. Molded parts to duplicate final design in questionable areas of durability.

b) Droptest parts. Same as above. Fabricated parts are not to be us ed for these applications.

13) Epoxy or Shell Rework

On contoured products where housing or body parts have to match the original pattern contour, duplicate in machinable epoxy or shells, made by the mold shop.

e.g. Door in doll body back for battery, or a deck lid on a hot wheel car.

14) T.V. and Catalog Picture Models

a) T.V. Models- For actors to use in making commercials, send model maker familiar with product to maintain model at studio, (He usually shows young actor how to use toy)

b) Catalog Picture Model- a finely finished shell for new Mattel catalog pictures.

15) Toy Show Models

Expensive durable working models our sales men use to sell the new toy line.

16) Salesmen Samples

Toys assembled on early run of engineering pilot using all available first shots, used on road by salesmen after toy show and left with the customer.

Product design model milestone summary #2

MATTEL MEMO

TO : Howard Newman

FROM : Eric Liddiard

DATE : May 27, 1967.

SUBJECT : Die-Cast Car Programme
(Telephone conversation, 26th May, 1967.)

OUR REF : ECL-1/67

The following is a brief restatement of the conversation this morning, please indicate by return mail if any of the following points of discussion were mis-understood. The major change in design concept is out-lined in the following manner.

To achieve the "California Styling" we will be required to use a 'Racing Slick' rear wheel. This will be the original 0.433 diameter but widened to 0.187. The front wheel will be 0.371 diameter with a width of 0.156. The effect of the dis-similar wheel diameter will give the styling a "Nose Down" appearance with the car body at approximately 2½ degrees to the road surface.

Later in the conversation we discussed wheel arch clearance and you had stated that the clearance should be 0.045 between wheel and car body, front and back, but to maintain the same clearance as used on the AMT 1/25 scale model. Upon studying our models and engineering lay-out, we find that to get sufficient clearance for a Racing Slick we are faced with the following alternatives :-

(a) We can lower the rear wheel centre line and make only slight modification to the wheel arch.

(b) We can maintain existing wheel base and tracking dimension and make a major modification to the styling of the wheel arch.

Jack Hargreaves is not enthusiastic about the first alternative as all his tooling epoxies are completed for the chassis, and it would mean a complete re-start for him and major modification on his epoxy work already completed on the bodies.

continued........

Early internal Mattel Hot Wheels memo

MEMORANDUM

TO: Floyd Schlau

May 24, 1967

FROM: Steve Wagner

RE: Miniature Car Project

This memorandum summarizes the discussions which we have had over the past several months with respect to three particular areas:

1. Method of Designing Prototype

We have discussed the method which Mattel will use to design the prototypes of the miniature cars which will be offered for sale. The question has arisen whether Mattel could encounter any problems if, in designing the prototypes, it utilizes models which have been produced by other model companies. I have advised you that if we use models manufactured by other companies (even for the purpose of pantographing) we could conceivably have a lawsuit filed against us on the grounds of unfair competition if such fact came to light. If such were to happen, the allegations would undoubtedly be that Mattel had taken the work product of another manufacturer and copied it. This could arise even though the other companies' models are not copyrighted. There is also a possibility that the other model makers may have design patents on their models, and if such is the case, an action alleging patent infringement could conceivably be instituted against Mattel. I, therefore, recommend that we do not utilize any models presently in existence which have been manufactured by other companies, but instead design our prototypes by utilizing drawings, designs and specifications which we have received from the domestic car producers such as General Motors and Ford.

2. Appearance of the Miniature Cars

I have recently been advised that Mattel is no longer interested in designing miniature cars which are exact replicas of the various production cars manufactured by General Motors and Ford. It has come to my attention that we are contemplating "souping up" our miniature cars by adding pipes, power domes, air intake scoops and possibly other items.

I feel that a short history of our negotiations with the various auto manufacturers is in order. We first commenced to discuss the possibility of manufacturing miniature cars in late December, 1966, or early January, 1967. In the middle of January, I sent letters to various persons in Chevrolet, Cadillac and GMC Divisions of General Motors, and a letter to Ford Motor Company. In

One of the earliest (if not *the* earliest) internal Mattel Miniature Car Project memos (Hot Wheels), dated May 24, 1967

Hand drawing of Sugar Caddy prototype concept #1 (1970)

Hand drawing of Sugar Caddy prototype concept #2 (1970)

Hand drawing of Pit Crew prototype concept #1(1970)

Hand drawing of Pit Crew prototype concept #2 (1970)

Hand drawing of early Power Pad prototype concept #1 (1970)

Hand drawing of early Power Pad prototype concept #2 (1970)

Early drawing of Side Kick, by Larry Wood (1970)

ADVERTISING ARTIST - OTTO KUHNI

Special Feature by: Bruce Pascal

Bruce Pascal of Washington, DC was born in 1961. When Mattel released the first Hot Wheels in 1968 Bruce was one of those kids playing with the tracks, accessories and racing cars. He even had a Hot Wheels trash can in his bedroom! Around 1971 he put his cars away in a wooden cigar box, only to be given them back by his mother cleaning the house in 1999. At that point, a "bell" went off - and he started running ads in newspapers to buy Hot Wheels. Researching former Mattel employees, he started collecting cars they personally had kept for years - prototypes. Twenty years later Bruce has one of the largest collections of older prototypes, written a book on his collection, and has appeared on numerous TV shows. Bruce.Pascal@cushwake.com

THE ~GROOVY~ ART BEHIND THE TOYS!

As a young child in the early 1960s I remember the joy of walking into a hobby store, and seeing walls lined with model kits, from manufacturers like AMT, Revell, IMC, Entex, Aurora, and many more. The colorful box art showed the coolest cars, but of course when you opened the boxes you got some cheap plastic parts! Then there were those large cardboard boxes holding the coveted Eldon or Tyco slot car sets with wonderful illustrations full of color, and showing the black race track and beautiful race cars. One can still remember that excited feeling of setting up the track and racing those super-fast slot cars with friends.

In 1968 Mattel introduced Hot Wheels, with cool new packaging that showed the actual Hot Wheels below a cool flame and race car graphic designed package. Then came the accessories with amazing box art showing kids playing with the Jump Ramps, Trestle Loops, Rod Runners, Collector Cases, and more.

Cox was another one of the big names in the hobby industry, well known for their miniature flying airplanes first produced in the early 1950s, and their later extensive line of model cars (1961-1996). The vast majority were powered by their small .049 gas engines. My favorites being the Dune Buggy and the Pinto (circa 1972).

Part of the manufacturers plans to get the kids to buy, or beg their parents to buy these toys was to utilize the best artwork possible on the box, because imagination was rampant with the young kids, and the goal was to get them excited! The artist who created the exciting box art for Tyco, and Eldon slot car sets, Mattel Hot Wheels, numerous model kits, Cox cars & airplanes, and many others was Otto Kuhni.

Otto was born in 1927 in Provo, Utah; the son of a school teacher who was also an artist. In 7th and 8th grade Otto took art classes, which inspired his artistic side. Funny side note, he learned to fly before he drove a car. In 1946 he joined the Navy and was a draftsman there. Once out of the Navy his first real job was drawing topographical maps for dams, roads and aqueducts. He then realized to be more successful he needed to move to Los Angles where he became a freelance artist. His list of clients was amazing: J. Walter Thompson, Max Factor, Lockheed, Tyco, Mattel, Lear, Playtime, Cox, Douglas, Entex, Garrett Aviation and too many more to list.

As a collector of Hot Wheels, I was anxious to find out who the artist of the Hot Wheels box art was; none of the box artwork Otto did ever had his signature, freelance artists were rarely given credit on toy boxes. But I was able to track him down about 15 years ago, discovering his name and phone number. A phone call followed, and he was excited to talk about his involvement with Hot Wheels and other toys. About a week later I mentioned to a contact at Mattel that Otto was alive and well, and they were happy to hear he was still painting. My contact said: "Ask him if he wants to come back." The answer was yes, and Otto returned to work for

their Redline Club line, and produced some of his best artwork ever over the next decade.

One story Otto told was of the car on the first Hot Wheels packages that came out in mid 1968. The blue car was not an actual recreation of any specific real car. Mattel management didn't want to pay royalties to a manufacturer, so he drew a car that looked like a blend of something from Dodge, Ford and GM. The beautiful Charger like car is gorgeous, too bad no manufacturer ever made it! In 2008, forty years after the "blue car" was first shown on the package Mattel made it into a Hot Wheels, and they named it the "Custom Otto." Then Mattel went one big step further, spending over $100,000 to create a one-of-a-kind diamond studded "Custom Otto" to use as their show piece for the 40th anniversary of their Hot Wheels line.

In 2012, Kuhni's Hot Wheels efforts got him elected in the Diecast Hall of Fame where he received the Diecast Designers Award.

Otto passed away in 2017, and left a legacy of artwork on toy boxes that will never be replicated. After his death I received a phone call from his family; remembering my friendship with Otto, they asked me if I was interested in acquiring all his artwork found in his house. I immediately flew to his home and negotiated the purchase of over 1,000 items. The collection contained pencil sketches of magazine covers, Hot Wheels posters, originals and printer's proofs of box art, oil paintings, and sketch pads. His art touched most all areas of transportation; airplanes, cars, boats, trains, and people were his subjects. Today his artwork sells from $100 for a small pencil sketch to pieces such as an original of "Battlestar Galactica" selling in a recent auction for over $5,000.

My goal is to eventually catalog his collective works, keep the Hot Wheels items, and let other collectors acquire his other works.

BP

Ed. note - Want to see more of Otto's art? Take a look at Bruce Pascal's terrific Hot Wheels website: hotwheelsonline.com

Mattel's $100,000 diamond studded "custom auto".

Editorial originally featured in AutoMobilia Resource magazine, a publication about automotive memorabilia. Resources can be found at www.AutoMobiliaResource.com

To contact Bruce Pascal visit

Redlineprotos.com

Hotwheelsonline.com

or email him at alpascal@aol.com

Follow on Instagram!
@pinkbeachbomb

www.ingramcontent.com/pod-product-compliance
Lightning Source LLC
Chambersburg PA
CBHW061756290426
44109CB00030B/2871

9780982500576